Ardelean Gheorghe Cornel(BIGAGC)

Book content:

Ardelean Gheorghe Cornel(BIGAGC)

Ardelean Gheorghe Cornel(BIGAGC)

Prologue

Efficient and effective activism action helps us achieve:

1. Personal goals
2. More successful
3. What we want in life
4. Obtaining and maintaining employment
5. Achieving and maintaining a happy marriage
6. Training and development of a personality as strong, beautiful and effective
7. Etc.

Only effective action helps us achieve success and personal goals.

Actions to be effective must be planned, organized correctly.

We through perseverance, will, efficiency, experience, theoretical knowledge effectively to achieve more and more action more effective and operational.

We must live as a personal goal as priority actions to achieve more effective and operative times.

Effective and positive activism helps a lot to achieve more effective and more positive action.

Effective positive actions and positive activism effectively helps us maintain health and prevent illness.

Positive activism effectively be supported, appreciated, respected and rewarded.

AGC ideas and thoughts in this book and others to come help a lot to achieve effective positive action to develop effective continuous positive activism and therefore to achieve personal goals and what we want in life.

Please write me how you have helped these ideas.

The money invested in this book of mine and the others that follow it is worth it, and it is almost nothing comparing to the pozitive efects that this book can have in your life, by applying the ideas to your life.

This volumes must be bought and used day by day, in order to development your personality and to the accomplish of all that you want.

These books contain lots of pozitive, optimist, creative, dinamic ideas, that push you to action, to thinking, things that are necesary your daily life and to accomplish your personal objectives.

Reading and analizing the ideas in this book and aplying them, we'll fiind solutions and ideas that will help us find:

I. To discover:

1. Qualities
2. defects
3. Capabilities
4. Qualifications
5. Some opportunities to succeed in life
6. Feelings
7. What we do to be loved
8. How to love
9. How to realize and maintain a true mutual love
10. How to realize and maintain a happy marriage
11. Mistakes, errors, wrong ideas
12. Etc.

II. To prevent some:

1. Divorces
2. Mistakes
3. Suspect
4. Griefs
5. Conflicts
6. Accidents
7. Failures
8. Bankrupstcy
9. Etc.

III. To become more:

1. Happy
2. Loved
3. Honored.
4. Appreciated,
5. wanted,
6. Optimistic,
7. Good,
8. Unselfish,
9. Emotional,
10. Altruists

11. Stronger
12. Efficient
13. Organized
14. Planners
15. Active
16. Honest
17. Human
18. Popular
19. Famous
20. Flexible
21. Adaptable
22. Understanding
23. Prompt
24. Etc.

IV. To get out of a state of:

1. Despair
2. Pessimism
3. Passiveness
4. Inactivity
5. Inefficiency
6. Inflexibility

7. Crisis

8. Inadaptability

9. Etc.

V. To participate more actively to:

1. Social life

2. Political life

3. Nonprofit organizations activities

4. Etc

VI. To participate more actively and efficiently in achieving true love and a happy marriage

VII. To find more likely situations conducive to achieving and maintaining a happy marriage life

VIII. To change our life for the better and to make it more beautiful

IX. To multiply and increase the chances to find your life partner

X. To raise and educate our children better so we can take better care of them

XI. Fiind more and bigger chances to meet favourable situations to accomplish and maintain a happy marriage for life.

XII.   Change our life in good and make it better.

XIII.   To multiply and increase the chances to find your life partner

XIV.   To raise and educate our children better so we can take better care of them.

I write and gather these thoughts, ideas in books, internet and other publications because these are useful to us every day and it is necessary to apply them to accomplish what we want, a better and beautiful life and propsperous.

These thoughts reflect a small part of what is good in reality and human relationships.

I wait to hear from you good news, good deeds that you have done influenced from what you have read from these books to make your life more beautiful, properous, happier and to be a pozitive example for others.

Each of us an become pozitive examples for others around us, participating to the creation of a better, prosperous and happier human society.

I'd be happy if one or more ideas read from these books helped you in a way or another and made you happier and prosperous.

Ardelean Gheorghe Cornel(BIGAGC)

I'm waiting to hear from you, your ideas and oppinions, your joys and griefes and your suggestions for new book subjects and i also appeal to your participation of promoting on the internet and mass media of the ideas and the books i've written.

I invite you to e-mail me at my email address: aradforex@gmail.com

Dear readers I wish you all health, happiness and achievement of all your wishes.

Best regards and respect,

Ardelean Gheorghe Cornel(BIGAGC)
981 Principal Street
Macea, Arad county
Zip Code 317210
Romania
Tel # (40) 0754652128

Accomplishing

1. A great capacity of accomplishing strategies of applying thinking on a big scale helps us become wise.

2. A great capacity of accomplishing strategies of applying thinking on a big scale helps us achieve more personal goals.

3. A great capacity of accomplishing strategies of applying thinking on a big scale helps us maintain our happiness.

4. A great capacity of accomplishing strategies of applying thinking on a big scale helps us maintain our way of being cautious.

5. A great capacity of accomplishing strategies of applying thinking on a big scale must be formed.

6. A great capacity of accomplishing strategies of applying thinking on a big scale helps us become more loved.

7. A great capacity of accomplishing strategies of applying thinking on a big scale helps us become more understanding.

8. A great capacity of accomplishing strategies of applying thinking on a big scale helps us maintain our optimism.

9. A great capacity of accomplishing strategies of applying thinking on a big scale helps us maintain our efficiency.

10. A great capacity of accomplishing strategies of applying thinking on a big scale helps us maintain our way of being practical.

11. A great capacity of accomplishing strategies of applying thinking on a big scale helps us maintain our humanity.

12. A great capacity of accomplishing strategies of applying thinking on a big scale helps us maintain our way of being loving

13. A great capacity of accomplishing strategies of applying thinking on a big scale helps us achieve more successes.

14. A great capacity of accomplishing strategies of applying thinking on a big scale must be rewarded.

Achievements

15.   When we are depressed it is necessary to get in contact with optimistic people and to do things which bring us success, achievements and hopes.

16.   Positive effective models, very useful to us, we find it necessary to look how they live: 1) studying as many biographies of people who have had great successes and achievements, 2) interviews and all that is written about people with success stories in the media and on the Internet; 3) direct discussion with people when we have successful opportunities, and continually seek to have the opportunity to discuss with people of success; 4) to work together with people of success; 5) through discussions with people who have known or worked with people of success; 6) with family members of successful people.

17.   Those who fail to escape the routine of everyday habits have inefficient behavior, are messy, slow, chaotic, etc. and they will have many failures and few and small achievements in life.

18. Those who are slaves to routine life and have many smaller or very big failures, usually small achievements and successes, personal and professional unfulfillments, they are in fact slaves of their own inefficient, clumsy behaviors which affect their efficiency, their quality of the future etc..

19. The knowledge given in schools to the people who attend them should include the achievements of science to day, not knowledge morally outdated.

20. The envy of the achievements of others is a very stupid thing.

21. The envy of the other achievements unnecessary to us consumes our very precious time.

22. The envy of the achievements of others is a very large flaw, you should remove it as soon as possible because it harms us greatly.

23. People with skills do not envy the achievements of others but appreciate them to just their value.

24. Envy for the achievements of others destroys us on the inside like cancer harming us very much.

25. Today unfortunately the people of the planet just use a tiny part of the conquests and the achievements of science.

26. Parents should be very careful with children and never forget to recognize all their positive achievements, to reward them in one way or another.

27. Dissatisfaction should push us towards our achievements, help us, push us to persevere for better results.

28. Parents need to be very careful with children and never forget to recognize their positive achievements, to reward them in one way or another.

29. Positive dissatisfaction of our achievements helps us, pushes us to persevere for better results.

30. Recognizing the achievements of people impels them to increase their efficiency.

31. Recognizing the achievements of people makes them loyal.

Actions

32. Proper planning of our actions increases our chances to achieve successes.

33. Despicable actions we are ultimately harmful to us.

34. Sly actions are short-lived until they are discovered.

35. Even if the sly actions can help us at a moment, they will harm us eventually.

36. Negative actions can help us at a moment, but they will harm us eventually.

37. Positive actions surely take us to larger or smaller successes, even if we realize them with bigger or smaller efforts.

38. People who fail to master their impatience are not received in certain actions.

39. Periodic analysis of our actions is very necessary to help us increase the effectiveness of future actions.

40. Positive actions should be taken as models.

41. Positive actions prevent many negative actions.

42. Positive actions should be appreciated.

43. We can prevent errors by better organizing our actions.

44. We can prevent errors through a better planning for our actions.

45. Popularization of positive actions is a necessity.

46. Preventive actions are very effective in most cases.

47. Aberrant actions lead us to failure.

48. Through positive actions we can prevent many failures.

49. The more skillful we are in our actions, the grater chances we have to succeed in those actions.

50. The self control of our actions is a required quality.

51. Success in actions is a result of many factors that are favorable to success.

52. Planning our actions is a factor of successes.

53. The effects of human actions have an increasing influence on the environment. This makes us think on a global scale, long-term and scientific before acting and makes us perform more profound studies, of impact, regarding our actions, to prevent the implementation of actions that have negative, inadmissible effects on the environment, society and people.

54. All employees of international organizations and states, which act during the performance of their duties with irresponsibility should be dismissed immediately and effective measures to recover the damage created by their irresponsible actions should be taken.

55. Women bring much in the life of a man, much joy, much happiness and satisfactions.

Activities

56. Spiritual self-development helps and contributes greatly to self-progress in other actions and activities.

57. The transparency of the institutions' activities prevents many acts of corruption.

58. We can encounter more easily favorable situations for us if we continue to focus on our activities.

59. Short-term thinking refers to short term projects, actions, activities, etc.

60. Thinking long term refers to long term projects, actions, activities.

61. Many who have bankrupted were also set up in a place where there were no commercial activities and then those who managed them did not know know to attract enough customers not to go bankrupt.

62. Involvement in positive activities helps us become more sociable.

63. Single people can get rid of loneliness when involved in positive activities.

64. We can form the quality of social activities through the Internet by participating in debates in forums, in the creation of a forum, when we communicate with other people.

65. Involvement in positive activities is a necessity for all of us.

66. We can remove the feeling of loneliness through our involvement in positive activities as much as possible.

67. The young love and want to participate in social activities.

68. Men cooperating in activities are more likely to maintain a happy marriage.

69. An intelligent man is cooperative in activities.

70. People who are used to carrying out the activities they have started have greater chances to achieve personal goals.

71. People who are used to carrying out the activities they have started have the capacity to achieve efficient co-developments.

72. The world does not provide the conditions necessary and mandatory for the activities necessary to achieve a performance in raising children and its importance.

73. People who are used to carrying out the activities they had started have a high capacity to achieve a happy life.

74. People who are cooperative in activities can contribute a lot to global humanization.

75. People who succeed in carrying out the activities they had started have greater chances to meet favorable situations.

76. People who succeed in carrying out the activities they had started have the capacity to achieve a more beautiful life.

77. A good state of health is an engine to achieving progress in all areas of activities.

78. The production of ideas is one of the most efficient human activities.

79. Efficient global co operations will form and develop many local activities in many places of the world.

80. A man who is cooperative during activities must be promoted, supported and rewarded.

81. A man who is cooperative during activities has more chances to participate in efficient global co operations.

Activism

82. It is necessary and required of young people to give proof of activism necessary in all that

affects them directly and indirectly, immediately, in medium or long term, more or less.

83. Activism maintains our health.

84. Activism is good for us.

85. Activism maintains our optimism.

86. Activism maintains our hopes and creates other hopes.

87. Activism must be efficient not only just exist.

88. In life, through passivity and lack of activism we can not progress.

89. Those who have big preferences for positive uncontrollable activism contribute a lot to many exchanges of information.

90. Those who have big preferences for positive uncontrollable activism have potential and great chances to achieve a true mature love.

91. Activism is the creator of success.

92. Activism makes our life more beautiful.

93. Activism helps us and contributes very much to have more opportunities to meet more favorable circumstances.

94. Activism helps us very much, and increases our chances of achieving personal goals.

95. Those who have high preferences for uncontrollable positive activism have a high potential of achieving a happy life.

96. Those who have high preferences for uncontrollable positive activism have the potential and big chances to achieve great outstanding performances.

97. Those with high preferences for unstoppable positive activism become more credible.

98. Those with high preferences for unstoppable positive activism become more efficient.

99. A nervous date reduces our activism.

100. Those who prefer unstoppable activism are a great engine of progress in all areas of activity.

101. Those who prefer unstoppable positive activism have potential and great chances to achieve a beautiful life.

102. The preference for uncontrolled positive activism must be appreciated, promoted, supported and rewarded.

103. Those who prefer uncontrolled positive activism have great chances and potential to become happy.

104. Those who prefer uncontrolled positive activism have an even greater power.

105. Those who prefer unstoppable positive activism have a great potential to succeed in life.

106. Those who have preferences for unstoppable positive activism have a great potential to succeed in life.

107. Those who prefer unstoppable positive activism have a great potential to achieve themselves.

108. Those who prefer unstoppable positive activism contribute to achieving global performances.

109. Those who have preferences for unstoppable positive activism achieve more efficient co operations.

110. The state of restlessness reduces a lot our activism.

111. The state of fatigue reduces a lot our activism.

Adaptable

112. Those who are remarkably gifted are adaptable.

113. We can prevent some failures also through the contribution of the formation, development, maintenance and usage of adaptable behaviors.

114. The force of our ideas can be enhanced also through the contribution of the formation, development, maintenance and usage of adaptable behaviors to situations that we must cope with.

115. Loneliness can be prevented also through the contribution of the formation, development, maintenance and usage of adaptable behaviors.

116. Sometimes love makes us more adaptable.

117. Our chances of becoming happy increase if we are adaptable.

118. In order to follow and transform our personal goals into reality, it is necessary to also form, develop, maintain and use our adaptable behavior.

119. Continuous self perfection helps us become adaptable.

120. Continuously making ourselves efficient helps us become adaptable.

121. Our own happiness can be achieved and maintained also through the contribution of the formation, development, maintenance and usage of adaptable behavior.

122. In order to prevent failures it is necessary to also form, develop, maintain and use adaptable behavior.

123. We can contribute to the achievement of our greatest accomplishments also through the contribution of the formation, development, maintenance and usage of adaptable behavior.

124. Confidence in ourselves helps us become adaptable.

125. Continuous self-control helps us become adaptable.

126. Acting efficiently helps us become adaptable.

127. In order to rise up once again for the first time for the who knows what time it is necessary to also form, develop, maintain and use adaptable behavior.

128. Our future can be projected and achieved also through the contribution of the formation, development, maintenance and usage of adaptable behavior.

129. The obstacles that prevent us from achieving our personal goals can be surpassed also through the contribution of the formation, development, maintenance and usage of adaptable behavior.

130. Wisdom helps us become adaptable.

131. Positive experience can be achieved also through the contribution of the formation, development, maintenance and usage of adaptable behavior.

132. Some mistakes can be prevented also through the contribution of the formation, development, maintenance and usage of adaptable behavior.

133. Our happiness depends a lot also on the formation, development, maintenance and usage of adaptable behavior.

Adequate

134. Prejudices are some inadequate ideas of reality.

135. Employers should be supported, encouraged by states to develop their business, to improve, in order to give adequate salaries.

136. Education that is inadequate is the direct or indirect cause of most crimes.

137. Weariness can be prevented through proper diet, education, positive behavior balanced intellectual exercise, perseverance, will, exercise, a value system that we believe in and that we respect, business dynamism, social relations, friends, mature love, a happy marriage, adequate rest when necessary, appropriate sleep, entertainment, etc.

138. Inadequate education is a major cause of the very many crimes.

139. Family violence results in very many cases from an inadequate education that has cultivated familiar violence.

140. Inadequate education makes a lot of us not achieve personal goals.

141. Inadequate education diminishes the number and quality of opportunities to encounter favorable circumstances.

142. If we change our inadequate ideas we can become even more efficient.

143. Inadequate education slows the achievement of personal goals.

144. Inadequate education reduces the number and quality of opportunities to find favorable situations.

145. Inadequate education is directly or indirectly the cause of most crimes.

Administration

146. Young people from each state are required to become those powerful engines of progress, in general, and progress in every field including social, public administration,

politics, as now they are not, unfortunately, in most of the world's states.

147. Young people from all states in the world who are marginalized, not taken into account, it is necessary to act, to be organized in NGOs, trade unions, political parties and other institutions, to act with efficiency and effectively to promote and support the rights and interests that their leadership is found in administration councils, local and central state, parliaments, local governments, etc..

148. There is incredibly much property in many states of the world. This is due to the inefficiency and the responsibility of state administration.

149. The effective administration of personal time increases our chances to achieve our personal goals.

150. The more efficient administration of our time help us to achieve personal goals more quickly.

Adverse

151. The depression of one of the spouses sometimes adversely affects family relationships.

152. Discrimination very much adversely affects the harmonious development of the personality of many children of the world's states.

153. Preventing premature actions helps us a lot more to prevent actions that adversely affect us and the others.

154. Using adverse events in our favor helps us achieve more favorable chances.

155. Using adverse events in our favor helps us achieve more records.

156. Using adverse events in our favor helps us achieve more favorable situations.

157. Using adverse events in our favor helps us achieve more pleasant surprises.

158. Using adverse events in our favor helps us achieve more efficient co operations.

159. Using adverse events in our favor helps us achieve more personal goals.

160. Using adverse events in our favor helps us achieve more true friendships.

161. Using adverse events in our favor helps us achieve more performances.

162. Using adverse events in our favor helps us achieve much good luck.

163. Using adverse events in our favor helps us achieve more successes.

Afraid

164. We can form courage and grow it by more positive, effective and planned behaviors. Among these are the continued developments of our knowledge in as many areas that can influence directly or indirectly our personal goals as possible. Usually, we are afraid to face the unknown. The longer we accumulate more knowledge we need in areas in which we act, the more we become more courageous, more confident in ourselves, with more success. Therefore, it is necessary, useful and mandatory to develop what we need because it has multiple positive effects on us, besides the fact that we continuously increase our

courage that we really need to achieve our personal goals.

165. If you have experienced failure you do not have to be afraid to continue what you started, if what you started was something positive.

Against

166. Discrimination is a great injustice done against those who are discriminated.

167. A grudge against another or others does not help us with anything in life.

168. Societies make "n" abuses against the unprotected, by not protecting them.

169. The society makes "n" abuses against the unprotected, by not protecting them.

170. The systems, the formal measures of the state made to solve human problems, the judicial system with certain behaviors typical to slave-owning, feudal, totalitarian, communist, inhuman, against man etc. societies. Many times in many situations people can decay morally, degrade mentally and physically, degrade their health, be an expert in crimes.

171. Any act of aggression against a family member by another family member is illegal and can be punished by the law.

172. The state's investment in an effective education that is against the obedience of the law is worth the effort, because if it is very effective with high-quality care it produces positive multiple and diverse effects recuperating the investments plus a large profit if you analyse in terms of financial efficiency the investment.

173. Family violence of the husband against the wife made the relationship between spouses deteriorate very much.

174. Local leadership in each city is necessary and must have as priority objectives, continuously, day by day, the fight against the excessive consumption of alcohol.

175. The prevention of each member of a family of all acts of aggression against another member of his family should be continuously, day by day a personal goal.

176. Men who are aggressive against a family member may change in behavior. Those who say they can not change in behavior

and they will not be aggressive towards one of the members of his family are wrong.

177. Even if someone does something wrong against us, we must not avenge them but respond kindly or we will make things worse.

178. When you are discriminated take all necessary measures to end discrimination and avoid the possiblity to get in a position to be discriminated against. You are not alone. Call institutions that are empowered. Good luck.

179. Life for many people would be more beautiful if they had not been discriminated against.

180. To succeed in life it is necessary to guard ourselves against negative influences.

181. To succeed in life it is necessary continuously, every day, for as long as we live, to have the personal goal to guard ourselves against negative influences.

182. A happy marriage is a shield against life's troubles.

183. It is required and necessary to have national fights against vices.

184. Any act of family aggression, made by a family member against another member of the family can not be reasoned and legally bound to be accepted under any circumstances.

185. Women who are aggressive against their family members may change their aggressive behavior to be a non-aggressive behavior in any family situation.

Agile

186. An agile man makes fewer mistakes.

187. An agile man has fewer failures.

188. An agile man succeeds to come out good from complicated situations.

189. An agile man knows how to prevent conflicts.

190. An agile man knows how to rapidly solve many problems.

191. An agile man knows how to prevent many arguments.

192. Positive personal objectives are faster and more easily and much faster achieved by those who are agile.

193. Resistance to change for the better can be defeated and overcome also through the formation, development, maintenance and usage of the ability to be agile.

194. Our resistance to change for the better can be defeated and overcome also through the formation, development, maintenance and usage of the ability to be more agile.

195. Love sometimes makes us more agile.

196. Communicative women have more chances to become more agile.

Allowing

197. By allowing what is bad can sometimes cause us much harm.

198. The power of not allowing ourselves to be stopped helps us achieve more records.

199. The power of not allowing ourselves to be stopped helps us achieve more favorable chances.

200. The willpower of not allowing ourselves to be stopped helps us achieve more performances.

201. The willpower of not allowing ourselves to be stopped helps us achieve more favorable chances.

202. The power of not allowing ourselves to be stopped helps us achieve more favorable situations.

203. The willpower of not allowing ourselves to be stopped helps us achieve more true friendships.

204. The power of not allowing ourselves to be stopped helps us achieve more true friendships.

205. The willpower of not allowing ourselves to be stopped helps us achieve more personal goals.

206. The power of not allowing ourselves to be stopped helps us achieve more personal goals.

207. The willpower of not allowing ourselves to be stopped helps us achieve more pleasant surprises.

208. The willpower of not allowing ourselves to be stopped helps us achieve much good luck.

209. The willpower of not allowing ourselves to be stopped helps us achieve more favorable situations.

210. The willpower of not allowing ourselves to be stopped helps us achieve more successes.

211. The willpower of not allowing ourselves to be stopped helps us achieve more records.

212. The power of not allowing ourselves to be stopped helps us achieve more successes.

213. The power of not allowing ourselves to be stopped helps us achieve more efficient co operations.

214. The willpower of not allowing ourselves to be stopped helps us achieve more efficient co operations.

215. The power of not allowing ourselves to be stopped helps us achieve more pleasant surprises.

Ambition

216. The people's ambition to act efficiently has contributed a lot to achieving the general good.

217. The ambitions man has a great potential to achieve efficient co operations.

218. Ambitions can be formed and developed.

219. People's ambition to act efficiently will lead to the achievement of many social relations.

220. People's ambition to efficiently act is achieved through a big exchange of information.

221. People's ambition to act efficiently helps us and contributes to a happy life.

222. People's ambition of acting efficiently helps them and contributes to continuously increasing their efficiency.

223. The ambition to act effectively that people have helps us contribute a lot to achieving a more beautiful life.

224. The ambition to act efficiently contributes a lot to success in life.

225. The ambition to achieve and act efficiently contributes a lot to achieving many efficient co operations.

226. The ambition to act efficiently of people helps them and contributes to achieving efficient co-developments.

227. Positive ambition is necessary.

228. Negative ambitions are very harmful sometimes.

229. Positive ambition must always be encouraged.

230. Positive ambition must always be appreciated.

231. Positive ambition must always be rewarded.

232. Positive ambition has helped enormously in the progress of mankind.

233. Positive ambition can be formed.

234. Positive ambition can be continuously developed.

235. Positive ambition has achieved many performances.

236. Positive ambition prevents many negative facts.

237. Maintaining positive ambition must be a personal objective of ours for as long as we live.

Analytic

238. The analytic spirit increases our chances and possibilities to achieve more successes.

239. The analytic spirit helps us a lot to prevent many mistakes.

240. The analytic spirit helps us a lot to prevent many failures.

241. The analytic spirit has a great contribution to achieving our success in life.

242. The analytics spirit increases our power.

243. Problems cannot be solved by the ideas that created them but through the contribution of the formation, development, maintenance and usage of analytic spirit.

244. In order to follow and transform our personal goals into reality, it is necessary to also form, develop, maintain and use our analytic behavior.

245. Confidence in ourselves helps us become analytic.

246. Problems cannot be solved by the ideas that created them but also through the contribution of the formation, development, maintenance and usage of analytic behavior.

247. Stress can be prevented also through the formation, development, maintenance and usage of analytic behavior.

248. Creativity helps us become analytic.

249. Aspiring towards a more meaningful life can also be achieved through the formation, development, maintenance and usage of analytic behavior.

250. Continuous self-motivation helps us become analytical.

251. In order to escape poverty it is necessary to also form, develop, maintain and use analytic behavior.

252. Obtaining more and greater successes can be achieved also through the contribution of the formation, development, maintenance, usage of an analytic behavior.

253. Hopes can be created also through the contribution of the formation, development,

maintenance and usage of analytic behavior.

254. The obstacles that prevent us from achieving our personal goals can be surpassed also through the contribution of the formation, development, maintenance and usage of analytic behavior.

255. Will helps us become analytic.

256. In order to escape poverty it is necessary to also form, develop, maintain and use an analytical thinking behavior.

257. The radical transformation for the better of our life can be achieved also through the formation, development, maintenance and usage of analytic behavior.

258. Acting efficiently helps us become analytical

259. Our own happiness can be achieved and maintained also through the contribution of the formation, development, maintenance and usage of analytic behavior.

260. Our happiness depends a lot also on the formation, development, maintenance and usage of analytic behavior.

261. In order to rise up once again for the first time for the who knows what time it is necessary to also form, develop, maintain and use analytic behavior.

Anticipative

262. People who have the ability to take rapid quality decisions also have an anticipative thinking.

263. Those who have no hopes, in order to create their hopes in the future; they need to form and developed their anticipative thinking.

264. In order to change our desire of changing it is really necessary to form, develop, maintain and use anticipative thinking.

265. We can prevent some mistakes also through the formation, development, maintenance and usage of anticipative thinking.

266. Aspiring towards a more meaningful life can be achieved also through the contribution of the formation, development, maintenance and usage of an anticipative life conception.

267. Those who have high objectives in life mostly have an anticipative thinking.

268. Those who have not succeeded in making a happy marriage up to a certain date, in order to succeed they need to form and develop an anticipative thinking.

269. We can broaden our horizon more or less also through the contribution of the formation, development, maintenance and usage of anticipative thinking.

270. We can broaden our horizon even more through the contribution of the formation, development, maintenance and usage of an anticipative conception of life.

Applying

271. By reading and applying the ideas of these books and magazines we will find more opportunities to assert ourselves

272. The chances to become happy can be found and read, by applying the ideas from these books and magazines.

273. Applying in practice many ideas from these books, magazines, etc. you will be able to achieve much easier, much faster and even more personal goals.

274. By applying one or more ideas from these books and magazines we expand opportunities for achieving our personal goals.

275. Those who are alone can get rid of loneliness by applying the principle of cooperation.

276. The exchange of information contributes to applying some useful information.

277. By reading and applying some meditations written by me, these help us educate and raise our children better.

278. By reading and applying some meditations written by me, we take more care of our children, of those that we love and of others.

279. Learning and applying strategies of achieving happiness do not require many efforts but many people do almost nothing to learn and apply them although they may help create their own happiness.

280. A happy marriage is achieved through continuous efforts, through searching, finding and applying the necessary knowledge of achievement.

281. A great capacity of accomplishing strategies of applying thinking on a big scale helps us become optimistic.

282. A great capacity of accomplishing strategies of applying thinking on a big scale helps us achieve more favorable situations.

283. A great capacity of accomplishing strategies of applying thinking on a big scale helps us become more cautious.

284. A great capacity of applying strategies of thinking big style helps us achieve more pleasant surprises.

285. A great capacity of accomplishing strategies of applying thinking on a big scale helps us become wise.

286. A great capacity of applying strategies of thinking big style helps us become more preventive.

Aspiring

287. Aspiring towards a more meaningful life can be achieved also through the contribution of the formation, development, maintenance and usage of an anticipative life conception.

288. Aspiring towards a more meaningful life can be achieved also through the contribution of the formation, development, maintenance and usage of a long term conception of life.

289. Aspiring towards a more meaningful life can be achieved also through the contribution of the formation, development, maintenance and usage of an objective conception of life.

290. Aspiring towards a more meaningful life can also be achieved through the contribution of the formation, development, maintenance and usage of the ability to continuously surpass ourselves.

291. Aspiring towards a more meaningful life can be achieved also through the contribution of the formation, development, maintenance and usage of an anticipative conception of life.

292. Aspiring towards a more meaningful life can also be achieved through the contribution of the formation, development, maintenance and usage of a long term conception of life.

293. Aspiring towards a more meaningful life can also be achieved through the formation,

development, maintenance and usage of an objective conception of life.

294. Aspiring towards a more meaningful life can be achieved also through the contribution of the formation, development, maintenance and usage of the ability to be calm in any stressing situation.

295. Aspiring towards a more meaningful life can be achieved also through the contribution of the formation, development, maintenance and usage of long term thinking.

296. Aspiring towards a more meaningful life can be achieved also through the formation, development, maintenance and usage of a realistic conception of life.

297. Aspiring towards a more meaningful life can be achieved also through the formation, development, maintenance and usage of the scientific conception of life.

298. Aspiring towards a more meaningful life can be achieved also through the formation, development, maintenance and usage of a responsible conception of life.

299. Aspiring towards a more meaningful life can be achieved also through the formation, development, maintenance and usage of a progressive conception of life.

300. Aspiring towards a more meaningful life can be achieved through the obtaining of more successes.

301. Aspiring towards a more meaningful life can be achieved also through the contribution of the formation, development, maintenance and usage of the ability to continuously surpass ourselves.

302. Aspiring towards a more meaningful life can be achieved also through the contribution of the formation, development, maintenance and usage of a creative conception.

303. Aspiring towards a more meaningful life can be achieved also through the contribution of the formation, development, maintenance and usage of humanist conception.

304. Aspiring towards a more meaningful life can be achieved also through the contribution of the formation, development, maintenance and usage of a preventive conception.

305. Aspiring towards a more meaningful life can be achieved also through the contribution of the formation, development, maintenance and usage of the ability to see and find favorable situations to achieve our personal goals.

Assuming

306. A great capacity of assuming the necessary risks for achieving personal goals helps us become productive.

307. A great capacity of assuming the necessary risks for success helps us become loved.

308. A great capacity of assuming the necessary risks for achieving personal goals must be used.

309. A great capacity of assuming the necessary risks for achieving great successes helps us become more loving.

310. A great capacity of assuming the necessary risks for success helps us maintain our humanity.

311. A great capacity of assuming the necessary risks for success helps us achieve more efficient co operations.

312. A great capacity of assuming the necessary risks for success helps us maintain our efficiency.

313. A great capacity of assuming the necessary risks for success helps us achieve more successes.

314. A great capacity of assuming the necessary risks for achieving great successes helps us achieve more favorable situations.

315. A great capacity of assuming the necessary risks for success helps us achieve more pleasant surprises.

316. A great capacity of assuming the necessary risks for achieving personal goals helps us become more preventive.

317. A great capacity of assuming the necessary risks for achieving great successes helps us become practical.

318. A great capacity of assuming the necessary risks for achieving great successes helps us become cautious.

319. A great capacity of assuming the necessary risks for achieving personal goals helps us become more loved.

320. A great capacity of assuming the necessary risks for success helps us achieve more records.

321. A great capacity of assuming the necessary risks for achieving personal goals helps us become more productive.

Attitudes

322. Young people of the world's states, unfortunately, do not use their capacities and qualities, skills, abilities, attitudes, knowledge, and the enormous energy that they have, their enthusiasm and optimism, which are positive things, the desire of affirmation and of making achievements in order to participate in the activity of communal, municipal, departmental, regional councils of counties, of parliaments, of governments, etc..

323. Young people from all of the world's states should not be negligent, careless, passive, inactive, non-participative in taking decisions that concern them, their present and future, but to take part in decision-making in local councils, central parliaments, governments and other state and non-state institutions, and use all their capacities, abilities, skills,

attitudes, knowledge, energy, commitment and desire to assert and achieve great deeds, to create a more humane, more righteous, more happy, with less trouble world.

324. Where necessary, it is good to change attitudes and behavior because only so we can achieve happiness.

325. It is always needed to develop capacities, skills, qualities and attitudes, but we need the development of our personality, it is necessary to have this as a personal objective.

326. The creative attitudes that we do not have we must form to help us become more creative.

327. We can create a beautiful life for ourselves if we have creative attitudes.

328. We should always prevent suicidal behavior, attitudes, ideas and thoughts.

329. The state is required to set up specialized services for the prevention and elimination of suicidal behaviors, attitudes, ideas and

thoughts in order to reduce to a maximum the possibility of suicides.

330. We can make our life more beautiful and if we have creative attitudes.

331. We always need to prevent suicidal behavior, attitudes, ideas and suicidal thoughts.

332. It is needed to establish specialized services for the prevention and elimination of suicidal behaviors, attitudes, ideas and thoughts to reduce to a maximum possible suicides.

333. Creative attitudes, qualities and capacities must be rewarded.

Audacious

334 In order to follow and transform our personal goals into reality, it is necessary to also form, develop, maintain and use our audacious behavior.

335. Acting efficiently helps us become audacious.

336. Creativity helps us become audacious.

337. The obstacles that prevent us from achieving our personal goals can be

surpassed also through the contribution of the formation, development, maintenance and usage of audacious behavior.

338. Will helps us become audacious.

339. Hope helps us become audacious.

340. The solutions to the problems we have or that we want to solve can be found also through the contribution of the formation, development, maintenance and usage of audacious behavior.

341. The limits of achievement imposed by ourselves in our mind at a given moment can be overcome or eliminated also through the contribution of the formation, development, maintenance and usage of audacious behavior.

342. Our resistance to changing for the better can be overcome also through the contribution of the formation, development, maintenance and usage of audacious behavior.

343. Continuously making ourselves efficient helps us become audacious.

344. Continuous self-motivation helps us become audacious.

345. Communication helps us become audacious.

346. Confidence in ourselves helps us become audacious.

347. Positive experience can be achieved also through the contribution of the formation, development, maintenance and usage of audacious behavior.

348. We can prevent the falling apart of a happy marriage also through the contribution of the formation, development, maintenance and usage of audacious behavior.

349. We can contribute to the achievement of our greatest accomplishments also through the contribution of the formation, development, maintenance and usage of audacious behavior.

Avoid

350. Through more reason for both sides to avoid many huge divorce.

351. There are more reasons for both sides to avoid many huge divorces.

352. Quarrels should always be avoided.

353. Making peace can avoid a lot of trouble.

354. We must avoid being careless.

355. We must avoid being superficial.

356. Many problems can be avoided by thinking positive.

357. Many problems can be avoided by the beliefs that we have.

358. Humanism contributes to avoiding more trouble.

359. Humanism contributes to avoiding many misdoings.

360. Wisdom helps us avoid many mistakes.

361. We can avoid evil most of the time if we act with maximum caution.

362. Large and small failures could be avoided if preventive thinking is used.

363. Many divorces could have been avoided if both spouses had had a preventive thinking.

364. Many problems can be avoided if we have a positive thinking.

365. Through an efficient and proper organization we can avoid many mistakes.

366. We can prevent more failures if we analyze our actions, their positive and negative effects, so that we and others achieve and avoid actions with negative, risky, illegal effects.

367. In any situation we find ourselves in, no matter how tough it is, we should avoid losing control.

368. Sometimes, our hastiness makes us make very big mistakes, with large negative effects, both for us and for others. So, beware, let us always avoid hastily behavior.

369. It is necessary and required to avoid blaming another or others for our mistakes.

370. Those with tact succeed in avoiding many arguments.

371. Those with tact succeed in avoiding misunderstandings, conflicts, arguments, annoyances within the family.

372. It is always necessary to avoid naggings regardless of the situation.

373. Lovers must always avoid argumentative talks.

374. Friends must always avoid argumentative talks.

375. Friends can avoid argumentative talks.

376. Spouses must avoid the apparition of new problems.

377. Spouses can avoid the apparition of new problems.

378. Mistakes can be avoided.

379. Mistakes must be avoided.

380. We can avoid mistakes by eliminating their causes.

381. Arguments must be avoided in any marriage.

Balanced

382. If we live a balanced life we are very likely to have a happy life.

383. If we live a balanced life we are very likely to have much more success than if we live an unbalanced life.

384. In order to achieve a balanced life is necessary to find a person to love and who loves us. Without a mutual happy love, we cannot have a balanced life.

385. A balanced life certainly leads us to happiness. It is worthwhile to make the necessary efforts to achieve a balanced life.

386. Weariness can be prevented through proper diet, education, positive behavior balanced intellectual exercise, perseverance, will, exercise, a value system that we believe in and that we respect, business dynamism, social relations, friends, mature love, a happy marriage, adequate rest when necessary, appropriate sleep, entertainment, etc.

387. A balanced marriage helps us a lot to achieve social relations.

388. Those who are emotionally balanced have a greater potential to contribute to the achievement of the greater good.

389. A balanced life prevents illness.

390. A balanced life helps us very much to keep our marriage happy.

391. A balanced life helps us get a lot more success.

392. A balanced life helps us keep our spiritual equilibrium.

393. A balanced life helps us protect our health.

394. A balanced marriage is also maintained with the help of positive exchanges of information.

395. Those who are emotionally balanced have a greater potential to succeed in life.

396. Balanced people have fewer failures.

397. A balanced marriage increases our trust in ourselves.

398. Those who are emotionally balanced have a greater potential to achieve their future.

399. A balanced marriage helps us a lot to achieve more and greater successes.

400. Those who are emotionally balanced have a greater potential to achieve efficient co operations.

401. We can contribute to achieving our happiness also through the contribution of

the formation, development, maintenance and usage of ideas to help us become balanced.

402. Those who are remarkably gifted are mostly balanced.

403. People who have not succeeded in achieving a happy marriage up to a certain date, in order to succeed they need to form and develop the necessary qualities to achieve and maintain a balanced love relationship.

Become

404. By acting, respecting the rules to becoming happy, we become happy

405. To become champions in a field it is necessary to act effectively by abiding by the rules which, if respected, make us champions.

406. It is never too late to become optimistic again.

407. Much more people can become happier and if much more of us determine, as on objective, to become happy.

408. Each of us has far greater opportunities to become more effective than we think.

409. Many of us can become happy much easier than we think we can.

410. Helping others to become happy is one of the priority objectives of my life.

411. Most of us could become happy if we set as a goal to become happy and if we act to achieve it.

412. We can become much more happy people if much more of us set as an objective becoming happier.

413. The chances to become happy can be found and read, by applying the ideas from these books and magazines.

414. Through cooperation we can become more prosperous more quickly.

415. Through cooperation we can become stronger more quickly.

416. Through cooperation we can become more popular more quickly.

417. Through co operation we can become invincible much faster.

418. Through co operation we can become more optimistic a lot sooner.

419. People can become happy if they have values that help them achieve their happiness.

420. Young people from each state are required to become those powerful engines of progress, in general, and progress in every field including social, public administration, politics, as now they are not, unfortunately, in most of the world's states.

421. We need to appreciate and support selfless ideas, to promote, to make them become facts.

422. The idea remains an idea; if not, it becomes a fact.

423. Day by day self-progress is necessary to become a personal objective, for as long as we live.

424. The science of raising children needs to become the object and subject of study in schools, universities, due to its importance.

425. As we become more credible we can more easily to establish more business relationships.

426. Sometimes some "nonsense" becomes a reality in time.

427. Some nonsense can be an absurdity for a period of time, after which it may become reality.

428. As we become more effective the more opportunities we have of achieving more successes.

429. The more effective we become, the more we have a greater chance to obtain greater and more successes.

430. If you know and apply the principles that lead us to happiness we are able to become happy.

431. Our objectives make us become more active.

432. Our objectives make us become optimistic or more optimistic.

Behavior

433. We can prevent greed by the self-control of our behavior.

434. Behavior for luxury is a big flaw.

435. Behavior for luxury can often lead to bankruptcy.

436. Behavior for luxury can be prevented by positive thinking.

437. Selflessness is a model of positive behavior that is necessary to appreciate.

438. We can prevent conceit by self-controlling our behavior.

439. Haughty behavior is very harmful to us.

440. Haughty behavior creates a distance for many people.

441. To envy others is a negative behavior.

442. Positive behaviors lead us to happiness.

443. The self-control of our behaviors can lead us to greater or smaller successes.

444. The more idols we have the more necessary it is that all our behaviors be positive.

445. All the educational institutions in the world need to form and develop unselfish thinking and selfless behavior.

446. Impatience is a behavior that can sometimes create very large disasters. For this reason it is necessary to prevent becoming impatient in inappropriate situations.

447. Envy is an incorrect behavior that damages us, and sometimes it can cause us enormously much damage.

448. Enmities are incorrect behaviors that damage, sometimes, both us, as well as those who are our enemies.

449. In life it is necessary and good to have behaviors that do not bring us enemies.

450. In any situation, no matter how difficult it would be, it is necessary to have a responsible behavior.

451. Sometimes, our hastiness makes us make very big mistakes, with large negative effects, both for us and for others. So, beware, let us always avoid hastily behavior.

452. Flexibility in thinking and behavior helps us achieve much easier, much faster and a larger number of personal goals.

453. Flexibility in thinking and behaviors helps us surpass many hard to overcome obstacles.

454. Flexibility in thinking and behaviors can be formed and developped if we do not have it.

455. Flexibility in thinking and behaviors is a quality necessary to achieve personal goals.

456. Flexibility in thinking and behaviors can be learned from those who have it.

457. Each of us must and needs to create other people's uncertainty by one's behaviors.

458. Shrewish behavior harms us.

459. Shrewish behavior often prevents a good understanding.

460. Shrewish behavior prevents harmony in a family.

461. Shrewish behavior can be prevented.

462. Brutality is a negative behavior that we can prevent.

463. Greed is a negative behavior that is necessary to prevent.

464. Unfortunately, society is not concerned enough, does not take the necessary measures to prevent the causes that lead certain people in a position where they need social protection and ensure the needed and obligatory human protection for people who need it.

465. Routine and daily habits should not be a brake for us, an impassable barrier in the form of our other more efficient, more orderly, faster, etc. behaviors.

466. Those who fail to escape the routine of everyday habits have inefficient behavior, are messy, slow, chaotic, etc. and they will have many failures and

467. We need to have the caution that it is necessary today to form and cultivate a cautious behavior.

468. When employees are wrong, leaders need to have normal reactions, a normal responsible behavior, and to consider that the employee who made a mistake and causes mistakes should take the necessary

steps to prevent other mistakes that may be made by the employee who made a mistake and by other employees.

469. Enthusiastic behavior greatly increases our opportunities to achieve personal goals.

470. The men thanked for their social behavior are likely to become more credible.

Beliefs

471. Many problems can be avoided by the beliefs that we have.

472. Some successes are the effects of beliefs.

473. The will of going against everyone else's beliefs helps us achieve more true friendships.

474. The strength of going against everybody's beliefs helps us achieve more favorable chances.

475. The strength of going against everybody's beliefs helps us achieve more personal goals.

476. The will of going against everyone else's beliefs helps us achieve more records.

477. The strength of going against everybody's beliefs helps us achieve more true friendships.

478. The strength of going against everybody's beliefs helps us achieve more performances.

479. The strength of going against everybody's beliefs helps us achieve more pleasant surprises.

480. The will of going against everyone else's beliefs helps us achieve more favorable chances.

481. The strength of going against everybody's beliefs helps us achieve more efficient co operations.

482. The strength of going against everybody's beliefs helps us achieve more favorable situations.

483. The will of going against everyone else's beliefs helps us achieve more successes.

484. The will of going against everyone else's beliefs helps us achieve more efficient co operations.

485. The strength of going against everybody's beliefs helps us achieve more records.

486. The will of going against everyone else's beliefs helps us achieve more performances.

487. The will of going against everyone else's beliefs helps us achieve more personal goals.

488. The will of going against everyone else's beliefs helps us achieve more favorable situations.

489. The will of going against everyone else's beliefs helps us achieve more pleasant surprises.

490. The strength of going against everybody's beliefs helps us achieve more successes.

491. The strength of going against everybody's beliefs helps us achieve much good luck.

Bold

492. There still are, unfortunately, in the XXI st century dignitaries in many countries which do not have any common sense, having the

boldness to hold their position that they can not cope with.

493. He who is bold has no common sense.

494. Those who have no sense are often also bold.

495. Good sense is not that of a bold man.

496. In order to prevent not achieving our personal goals, it is necessary to also form, develop, maintain and use our bold behavior.

497. Some mistakes can be prevented also through the contribution of the formation, development, maintenance and usage of bold behavior.

498. Our own happiness can be achieved and maintained also through the contribution of the formation, development, maintenance and usage of bold behavior.

499. In order to escape poverty it is necessary to also form, develop, maintain and use bold behavior.

500. The obstacles that prevent us from achieving our personal goals can be

surpassed also through the contribution of the formation, development, maintenance and usage of bold behavior.

501. Confidence in ourselves helps us become bold.

502. Acting efficiently helps us become bold.

503. Rather than lamenting that we do not have successes it is more useful to also form, develop, maintain and use bold behavior.

504. The force of our ideas can be augmented also through the contribution of the formation, development, maintenance and usage of bold behavior.

505. Self-imposed discipline helps us become bold.

506. Optimism helps us become bold.

507. Pessimism can be removed and replaced with optimism also through the contribution of the formation, development, maintenance and usage of bold behavior.

508. The limits of achievement imposed by ourselves in our mind at a given moment can be overcome or eliminated also through

the contribution of the formation, development, maintenance and usage of bold behavior.

Boundaries

509. A great capacity of continuously overcoming boundaries helps us maintain our optimism.

510. A great capacity of continuously overcoming boundaries helps us become understanding.

511. A great capacity of continuously overcoming boundaries helps us achieve more pleasant surprises.

512. A great capacity of continuously overcoming boundaries helps us become more humane.

513. A great capacity of continuously overcoming boundaries helps us become more enthusiastic.

514. A great capacity of continuously overcoming boundaries must be supported.

515. A great capacity of continuously overcoming boundaries helps us achieve more favorable chances.

516. A great capacity of continuously overcoming boundaries helps us become more practical.

517. A great capacity of continuously overcoming boundaries helps us maintain our productivity.

518. A great capacity of continuously overcoming boundaries helps us maintain our way of being understanding.

519. A great capacity of continuously overcoming boundaries helps us maintain our wisdom.

520. A great capacity of continuously overcoming boundaries helps us become more tolerant.

521. A great capacity of continuously overcoming boundaries helps us maintain our enthusiasm.

522. A great capacity of continuously overcoming boundaries helps us become tolerant.

523. A great capacity of continuously overcoming boundaries helps us maintain our way of being loved.

524. A great capacity of continuously overcoming boundaries must be encouraged.

525. A great capacity of continuously overcoming boundaries helps us become happier.

526. A great capacity of continuously overcoming boundaries helps us become productive.

527. A great capacity of continuously overcoming boundaries must be rewarded.

Calculated

528. Each of the spouses need to always be calculated in family relations in order to prevent arguments, conflicts, misunderstandings etc..

529. Calculated people have much greater opportunities to achieve more successes.

530. Calculated people are more likely to achieve much more of their personal goals.

531. Calculated people are more likely to encounter much more favorable circumstances.

532. Calculated people are more likely to become more efficient.

533. Calculated people are more likely to achieve happy marriages.

534. Calculated people are more likely to raise and to properly educate children.

535. The calculated man makes fewer mistakes or none at all.

536. The calculated man manages to accomplish smaller or greater successes.

537. Most calculated men manage to achieve happy marriages.

538. Most calculated men manage to maintain efficient co operations.

539. Most calculated people manage to make much more chances to meet more favorable situations.

540. Calculated people succeed in achieving efficient co-developments.

541. Calculated people besides calculation also develop other skills.

542. Calculated people manage to make friends a lot easier.

543. Calculated men participate in changing the world for the better.

Capacities

544. Our ability to create ideas can continuously increase for as long as we live, thus

increasing its value on a continuous basis. Our ability to create ideas affects us enormously in our achievement and maintenance of our happiness every day in every situation.

545. One of the objectives of each personal man is necessary and should be the continuous development as much as the ability to create useful, efficient, positive, humane ideas, which can contribute to the achievement of our personal happiness and maintain it.

546. As we grow with a grater ability to create positive, effective ideas, necessary to us, the more and more surely we can achieve personal goals and happiness and we can maintain them.

547. The ability to produce positive effective ideas, necessary to us is enormously useful and effective as it helps establish, develop, maintain other capacities as well which we can exemplify: 1) the ability to prevent mistakes and failures, 2) the ability to solve problems, 3) our ability to create and maintain happiness; 4) our ability to create, select, set and achieve personal goals; 5) our professional ability, 6) the ability to face

any blows of life as big and as painful as they would be; 7) the ability to create and maintain a family, a happy marriage.

548. The ability to produce positive effective ideas can increase greatly, easily and with minimum expenditure, with the help of the Internet, knowledge, positive models, which we can find using the Internet.

549. Until the creation and development of science and broadcasting them in an easy way for each, which includes the ability to create positive effective ideas, necessary to us, respectively the creation of science, the creativity of each of us, it is necessary to look in the edited books, in the media and on the Internet, whenever existing knowledge is needed.

550. As we have more capacities and qualities, the more chances we have to meet several favorable occasions.

551. Creative attitudes, qualities and capacities must be rewarded.

552. Those who control circumstances have more capacities of achieving more and greater successes.

553. Those who willingly expand their positive experience have greater capacities to efficiently co-develop.

554. Those who control circumstances have greater capacities to participate in achieving the greater good.

555. Our necessary capacities including those necessary to the achievement of personal objectives can be formed, developed, maintained and used through the contribution of the formation, development, maintenance and usage of the ability to efficiently organize.

Careful

556. Life would have much less trouble if we would be more careful in every action of ours.

557. We can prevent many unpleasant surprises if we are also sufficiently careful in everything we do and think.

558. Greed has led many people to bankruptcy, so be very carefully and prevent getting greedy.

559. Those who are careful have fewer failures.

560. Those with the sense of efficiency are more careful.

561. Careful people must be rewarded.

562. Careful people have greater chances to maintain mature love.

563. Sometimes our so-called true friends can get us in the biggest troubles possible, can sleep with our wife or with our husband, with our girlfriend or boyfriend, can take away our business, etc. Look around you. Be very careful for the so called true friendship.

564. True friendship is formed and maintained very difficultly and can break in a second. So be very careful. Do not play with it.

565. We can prevent negative actions if we are more careful in what we do.

566. Parents should be very careful with children and never forget to recognize all their positive achievements, to reward them in one way or another.

567. We can make our life more beautiful if we are always careful.

568. Illegal actions can destroy mature, true love. Is it worth it? No. So be careful.

569. Be careful in life at what is worth and not worth doing.

570. The states' institutions need to manage the public money more carefully, more efficiently, more responsibility because now this leaves much to be desired.

571. Parents need to be very careful with children and never forget to recognize their positive achievements, to reward them in one way or another.

572. Fear makes us be more careful.

573. Human mind is diabolical, it can achieve positive incredible facts, but unfortunately also facts that may be enormously, incredibly negative. So be careful, a man can do what an angel can, but at the same time he can do what the devil can too.

574. Careful people must be appreciated.

575. Careful people have more and greater chances to achieve more and greater successes.

576. Careful people make fewer mistakes.

577. People who are in love are sometimes less careful.

578. We need to be permanently careful at how we order and reorder our priorities of personal goals.

579. People who are careful must be supported.

580. People who are careful have more and greater chances to achieve true friendships.

581. People who are careful have more chances to achieve a mature love.

582. People who are not careful with others should not be rewarded.

Cautious

583. Sometimes, happiness makes us not be sufficiently cautious.

584. If women are more cautious, they could prevent much more divorces.

585. Caution in marriage helps us enormously to avoid conflicts, arguments, hate, distrust and sometimes even divorce. The more each of the spouses is cautious the better it is.

586. Caution and the art of being cautious is a part of wisdom that is good, useful, but necessary and required to continuously develop and apply it always where it is necessary in life.

587. If we have one or more failures we should not become scared but more cautious.

588. We need to have the caution that it is necessary today to form and cultivate a cautious behavior.

589. Failures make us more cautious.

590. A man who knows how to self portray himself is cautious.

591. A man's need for safety makes many people be more cautious.

592. Our chances of becoming happy increase if we are cautious.

593. Wisdom helps us become more cautious.

594. Will helps us be cautious.

595. Inter-human communication sometimes helps us become more cautious.

596. Mutual trust helps us become more cautious.

597. A great capacity of analyzing a situation logically helps us become cautious.

598. A great capacity of managing life helps us maintain our way of being cautious.

599. A great capacity of using available knowledge helps us maintain our way of being cautious.

600. A great capacity of being understanding with people helps us become cautious.

601. A great capacity of dealing with pressures, no matter how great they are, helps us maintain our way of being cautious.

602. A great capacity of being understanding with people helps us become more cautious.

603. A great capacity of anticipating helps us maintain our way of being cautious.

604. A great capacity of using qualities helps us maintain our way of being cautious.

605. A great capacity of achieving what was proposed helps us become more cautious.

606. A great capacity of making people more optimistic helps us maintain our way of being cautious.

607. A great capacity of understanding others helps us become cautious.

608. A great capacity of adopting visions helps us maintain our way of being cautious.

609. Confidence in ourselves helps us become cautious.

610. A great capacity of remaining involved in the same area with even greater objectives helps us maintain our way of being cautious.

611. A great capacity of using qualities helps us become cautious.

612. A great capacity of being convincing helps us become cautious.

613. A great capacity of encouraging people helps us become cautious.

Chance

614. Proper planning of our actions increases our chances to achieve successes.

615.   Usually, many of us use our time much more inefficiently than we have the chance and this is a very big mistake.

616.   Each of us has the chance to assert oneself in real life. It is important to discover the chances and to achieve the goal.

617.   The ideas of these books, magazines help us discover opportunities and the potential chances of life.

618.   The chances to become happy can be found and read, by applying the ideas from these books and magazines.

619.   The more skillful we are in our actions, the grater chances we have to succeed in those actions.

620.   Those who will consider wise pieces of advice will have more chances of success.

621.   The more objective we are, the more chances we have to be happy.

622.   Those who have a preventive thinking have more chances to realize their personal goals than those who do not have a preventive thinking.

623. Those who will consider positive pieces of advice will have more chances to achieve more performances.

624. The more positive and humane deeds we accomplish, the more we increase our chances of being happy.

625. As we develop more skills, the more and bigger chances we have to achieve personal goals. So, it is worth and it is necessary to develop and shape all the skills that we need in order to achieve personal goals.

626. The better we know ourselves, the more chances we have to relaunch our personal goals.

627. The more skillful we are in our actions, the more chances we have to obtain success in those actions.

628. We have more chances to keep a love relationship for a longer period of time if we are fair with each other.

629. Persons with many qualities have very big chances to achieve successes.

630. As we have more friends, the more chances we have to meet several favorable occasions.

631. As we have more capacities and qualities, the more chances we have to meet several favorable occasions.

632. As we have more co operations, the more chances we have to meet favorable occasions.

633. As we have more and diversified experience, the more chances we have to meet several favorable occasions.

634. The more developed personality we have, the more chances we have to meet several favorable occasions.

635. As we know more languages, the more chances we have to meet several favorable occasions.

Choices

636. The choices that we make day by day are at the same time an equally big number of positive chances, but, unfortunately, they are also a great number of ill fortunes.

637. The choices we can make continuously, day by day grow also due to the development of knowledge.

638. The choices we can make grow very much if we know a foreign language out of the ones that are more spoken.

639. The choices we can make increase very much if we have more personal goals to achieve.

640. The more informed and documented we are the more chances we have to identify more choices that we can make.

641. The more qualities we have the more chances we have to meet more choices that we can make.

642. Efficient co-developments increase our chances to meet more choices that we can make.

643. It is necessary to form and developed the science of making choices that are most adequate.

644. The science of making adequate choices helps you enormously in achieving more and greater successes.

645. The science of making the most adequate choices helps us become even more efficient.

646. The more credible we are the more chances we have of meeting more possibilities of choices that we can make.

647. Efficient co operations increase our chances of meeting more choices to be made.

648. The sense of making the right choices will help us greatly in achieving more and realizing personal objectives.

649. The science of making the right choices helps us a lot to have more chances to meet more favorable situations.

650. The choices we make are taken according to the values we have.

651. Our choices influence enormously our success or failure.

652. We can continuously make our choices more effective.

653. Effective choices can be formed.

Circumstances

654. Sometimes, the discriminated one in a given situation, may discriminate in other circumstances or situation.

655. Non-discrimination is a principle that every one of us must act to respect it in all circumstances.

656. There are circumstances in which, for certain news, accomplishments, etc. we can feel happy, but we can not be fully happy, for some reason, for example, because someone close to us has died.

657. True friends are those who wish you well, cooperate with you when you need to, who are there by your side in every good and bad situation. They are those people who do not leave in exceptional circumstances, the most difficult ones of your life.

658. There are certain situations in marriage when women have more and more qualities and greater achievements than men. In these circumstances the man should not feel inferior, complexed, frustated, moody, disturbed by the situation, etc.. but instead he should see the good side of the situation,

to enjoy a lot of the qualities and achievements of his wife, to be proud of her, to stimulate, appreciate and respect her more and assist her in achieving her objectives, to help her when she need his help and he can give it to her.

659. Many people in life have favorable circumstances but do not know how to use them in their favor.

660. People who live in favorable circumstances also use them in life to achieve more bigger or smaller successes.

661. It is necessary that each of us learns to see favorable circumstances and to use them in our favor.

662. In life, we have much more favorable circumstances if we have knowledge in many different areas. Because this is necessary for our own good to accumulate as long as we live as much knowledge in many areas as we can.

663. The more we search and the more useful theoretical efficient knowledge we find that are necessary in achieving our personal

goals, the more we discover more favorable circumstances for us.

664. The more creative qualities we have and the greater capacity of creation, the more we can find and discover more favorable circumstances for ourselves.

665. Some successes are due only to the qualities and exceptional efforts of people without the participation of any favorable circumstances.

666. Constructive thinking helps us and contributes greatly to the increasing number of opportunities to meet more favorable circumstances.

667. Cooperative behavior helps us have more opportunities to meet more favorable circumstances.

668. Creative behavior helps us have many more opportunities to meet more favorable circumstances.

669. Those who have more skills have more opportunities to encounter much more favorable circumstances.

670. Calculated people are more likely to encounter much more favorable circumstances.

671. Effective co operations increase our chances to meet more favorable circumstances.

672. Spiritual self-development done continuously, day by day, for as long as we live greatly increases our chances to have more opportunities to meet much more favorable circumstances.

673. Some successes are due mostly to favorable circumstances and a lot less to people.

674. The Internet helps us have more chances to meet much more favorable circumstances.

675. The world must legislate the obligation of putting recordings on the Internet of court sentences, of all documents related to the process, files, everything that is public information, except the circumstances stipulated by law when sentences are not public.

676. Those who control circumstances are engines of progress in all areas of activities.

Concentrating

677. Concentrating our energies helps us very much to meet more favorable situations.

678. Concentrating our energies helps us prevent many failures.

679. Concentrating our energies helps us a lot to achieve personal goals.

680. Concentrating on what we do helps us a lot to achieve more and greater successes.

681. Concentrating to a maximum contributes to everything that is necessary to do; it helps us continually increase our efficiency.

682. Concentrating our energies contributes a lot in achieving a happy marriage.

683. Concentrating our energies helps us achieve more and greater performances.

684. Concentrating our energies helps us and contributes a lot to achieving a happy life.

685. Concentrating our energies helps us a lot to find the right partner for life.

686. Concentrating our energies increases our credibility.

687. Concentrating our energies helps us achieve more and greater successes.

688. Concentrating our energies helps us achieve a mature love a lot easier.

689. Concentrating our energies helps us become even more efficient.

Consequent

690. Stress can be prevented also through the formation, development, maintenance and usage of consequent behavior.

691. Wisdom helps us become consequent.

692. Our future can be projected and achieved also through the contribution of the formation, development, maintenance and usage of consequent behavior.

693. Communication helps us become consequent.

694. We can overcome the difficulties that we must overcome also through the help of the formation, development, maintenance and usage of consequent behavior.

695. Obtaining more and greater successes can be achieved also through the contribution of the formation, development, maintenance, usage of a consequent behavior.

696. We can form, develop and maintain the state of being ourselves also through the contribution of the formation, development, maintenance and usage of a consequent behavior.

697. Some mistakes can be prevented also through the contribution of the formation, development, maintenance and usage of consequent behavior.

698. Rather than lamenting that we do not have successes it is more useful to also form, develop, maintain and use consequent behavior.

699. Will helps us become consequent.

700. The obstacles that prevent us from achieving our personal goals can be surpassed also through the contribution of the formation, development, maintenance and usage of consequent behavior.

701. Optimism helps us become consequent.

702. We can contribute to the achievement of our greatest accomplishments also through the contribution of the formation, development, maintenance and usage of consequent behavior.

703. Hopes can be created also through the contribution of the formation, development, maintenance and usage of consequent behavior.

704. The self efficient use of our time helps us become consequent.

705. The solutions to the problems we have or that we want to solve can be found also through the contribution of the formation, development, maintenance and usage of consequent behavior.

Constant

706. Those who constantly seek to find solutions to change their lives for the better will find more solutions.

707. Morale should be keept constantly, every day, for as long as we live, at its best.

708. Love is a dynamic process, constantly transforming itself.

709. Constantly, every day, continuously, for as long as we live it is necessary to have as a personal goal the harmonious development of our personality.

710. Good morale needs to be kept constant, every day, for as long as we live.

711. Our happiness depends a lot on the formation, development, maintenance and usage of the ability to constantly choose correctly.

712. Our mind can be constantly maintained young.

713. In order to follow and transform our personal goals into reality, it is necessary to also form, develop, maintain and use our constant behavior.

714. The limits of achievement imposed by ourselves in our mind at a given moment can be overcome or eliminated also through the contribution of the formation, development, maintenance and usage of constant behavior.

715. Obtaining more and greater successes can be achieved also through the contribution of

the formation, development, maintenance, usage of a constant behavior.

716. The obstacles that prevent us from achieving our personal goals can be surpassed also through the contribution of the formation, development, maintenance and usage of constant behavior.

Constructive

717. Constructive thinking was, is and will be irreplaceable in the development of our personality.

718. In life it is necessary and required to be able to have that personal goal as we continue the development of constructive thinking.

719. When we think constructively not destructively, we think this helps us prevent many mistakes, failures, accidents, divorces, misfortunes, conflicts, which are bad, harmful to us or others.

720. All those who have achieved in life more bigger or smaller successes mostly had a constructive thinking.

721. Constructive human relations, effective, harmonious ones help us greatly to achieve a beautiful life.

722. The longer we are able to achieve more constructive human relationships, effective, harmonious ones, of mutual confidence, the more we will succeed more, the more certain we are to have a harmonious happy life, with more satisfactions, joy, successes and much happiness.

723. Unfortunately in the world there are still far fewer constructive relations, effective, harmonious, mutual trust ones, compared to how many there could be.

724. Constructive ideas contribute to the achievment of personal goals.

725. Constructive ideas must take the place where destructive ideas are.

726. The competition must use only constructive ideas.

727. Constructive ideas also help contribute to achieving effective co operations.

728. It is necessary that every day, continuously, for as long as we live, to be influenced by positive constructive influences.

729. Constructive influences help us greatly to the achievement of our personal goals.

730. Constructive ideas help us achieve performance.

731. Constructive ideas can help us achieve success.

732. Constructive ideas help us contribute to becoming effective.

733. Constructive thinking is part of positive thinking.

734. Constructive thinking is needed to take the place of destructive thinking where there is any.

735. Thinking constructively contributes greatly to achieving personal goals.

736. Constructive thinking helps us and contributes greatly to the increasing number of opportunities to meet more favorable circumstances.

737. Constructive thinking is a factor that contributes greatly to maintaining a happy marriage.

738. Hopes are very constructive.

739. Trade unions should have only a constructive role in everything they do.

740. Trade unions must participate constructively, work with the management to streamline employment, to solve problems for working people and companies in order to prevent bankruptcy, unemployment.

741. Constructive ideas also help us keep our marriage happy.

742. Each parent is necessary and required to form and develop every child's constructive thinking since they are little.

743. Constructive thinking helps us greatly increase the efficiency of the use of our time.

Continually

744. Spouses need to continually build and develop the skills necessary to creating and maintaining a happy marriage.

745. Phisical self-development and maintenance, continually, day by day, is necessary to be achieved.

746. As a personal goal, for as long as we live, it is necessary and required to have both physical self-development and maintenance, continually, day by day.

747. Those who continually seek solutions to change their lives for the better will really be able to change it.

748. In life for as long as we live it is necessary, but also madatory that we continually expand our inner potential and this should be a primary and continuous objective.

749. Many of us still use our time more inefficiently than we can. Each of us has very large reserves and resources to greatly expand the effectiveness of using our time and we should use them to continually expand the efficiency of our time.

750. To increase the number of people who will set as a personal goal the spiritual self-development and who will create greater opportunities for spiritual self-development to be done by as many people as possible

who aimed for self-development as a personal goal, it is necessary to continuously create and develop the science of personal development which encompasses the spiritual and scientific personal self-development. Until we create and develop the science of spiritual development it is necessary to develop the science of spiritual self-development because so many people from many countries are more active and effective than the countries in which they live and thus they can be models for other people with positive models of personal self-development and so they can help them create and develop, achieve their personal objectives.

751. Unfortunately, at present there is no science of spiritual development, no science of spiritual self-development, and there are not many people who have set the objective of personal spiritual self-development, although spiritual self-development is extremely necessary and very useful to each person and society as a whole. Because of these shortcomings and large utilities for its individual and society, it is very useful and very necessary that as many people as

possible establish as a goal the personal self-development and have personal dedication to this goal for as long as they live to achieve themselves continuously and not wait until society or certain private or state institutions will create the science of spiritual development and the science of spiritual self-development.

752. Spiritual self-development will help us greatly in spiritual development that can be accelerated if we continually study the issues that can help us grow spiritually, issues that we find stored in books, publications, television, on the Internet, in the life experience of people who have values and ethics and have achieved many and great successes thanks to the development of their spirituality and ethic. The longer we self-develop spiritually the more opportunities we have to achieve more and greater successes that are made by spiritual self-development.

753. Positive effective models, very useful to us, we find it necessary to look how they live: 1) studying as many biographies of people who have had great successes and achievements, 2) interviews and all that is

written about people with success stories in the media and on the Internet; 3) direct discussion with people when we have successful opportunities, and continually seek to have the opportunity to discuss with people of success; 4) to work together with people of success; 5) through discussions with people who have known or worked with people of success; 6) with family members of successful people.

754. It is required to have as a personal goal the prevention of chronic fatigue, continually, day by day, for as long as we live.

Courage

755. A great capacity of drawing attention must be encouraged.

756. A great capacity of using available knowledge must be encouraged.

757. A great capacity of creating one's own safety must be encouraged.

758. A great capacity of making great plans must be encouraged.

759. A great capacity of being convincing must be encouraged.

760. A great capacity of being wise must be encouraged.

761. A great capacity of establishing great personal goals must be encouraged.

762. A great capacity of fighting back must be encouraged.

763. A great capacity of teaching people must be encouraged.

764. A great capacity of being creative in order to solve great problems must be encouraged.

765. A great capacity of using each failure to achieve successes must be encouraged.

766. A great capacity of preventing situations of being deceived must be encouraged.

767. A great capacity of establishing high personal goals must be encouraged.

768. A great capacity of learning in order to achieve successes must be encouraged.

769. A great capacity of achieving human relationships must be encouraged.

770. A great capacity of doing what is best must be encouraged.

771. A great capacity of using a value system must be encouraged.

772. A great capacity of having an even more energetic life must be encouraged.

773. A great capacity of enjoying work must be encouraged.

774. A great capacity of encouraging people must be encouraged.

775. A great capacity of anticipating must be encouraged.

776. A great capacity of gathering our energies must be encouraged.

777. A great capacity of using each injustice received in order to achieve successes must be encouraged.

778. A great capacity of making people more optimistic must be encouraged.

779. A great capacity of self-surpassing must be encouraged.

780. A great capacity of using available ideas must be encouraged.

781. A great capacity of using qualities must be encouraged.

782. Perseverance must be encouraged.

783. A great capacity of maintaining a positive efficient own lifestyle must be encouraged.

Decisions

784. People who have the ability to take rapid quality decisions must be appreciated.

785. People who have the ability to rapidly take quality decisions have more and greater chances to meet more favorable situations.

786. People who have the ability to take rapid quality decisions contribute more to global humanization.

787. Those who do not have hopes, in order to create hopes for the future need to connect with people who have the ability to rapidly take policy decisions.

788. People who know how to take quality decisions have long term thinking.

789. People who know how to take quality decisions are engines of progress in all areas of activity.

790. People who know how to take quality decisions are enterprising.

791. People who know how to take quality decisions contribute to developing a constructive life conception.

792. People who have the ability to take rapid quality decisions also have an efficient thinking.

793. People who have the ability to rapidly take quality decisions have more and greater chances to achieve more and greater successes.

794. People who know how to take quality decisions also have a preventive thinking.

795. People who know how to take quality decisions have a greater ability to achieve themselves.

796. Taking quality decisions is a necessity.

797. People who know how to take quality decisions have a greater ability to succeed in life.

798. People who know how to take quality decisions have a greater ability to achieve a mature love.

799. People who know how to take quality decisions have a greater ability to achieve efficient co-developments.

800. People who know how to take quality decisions have a greater capacity of avoiding possible failures.

801. People who know how to take quality decisions develop their life.

802. Those who know how to take quality decisions have much more chances of finding the right partner for life.

803. In order to take correct decisions we need to form, develop, maintain and use the ability to solve problems legally.

804. Emancipation from self imposed restrictions can be made through the formation, development and maintenance of the ability to take rapid quality decisions.

805. Forming wrong ideas can be prevented also through the formation, development,

maintenance and usage of the ability to take rapid quality decisions.

806. In order to take correct decisions it is necessary that we form, develop, maintain and use the ability to be responsible.

807. In order to pursue and transform our personal goals into reality we need to form and develop the ability to take rapid quality decisions.

808. In order to take fair decisions we must dissociate emotions.

809. The state of psychical discomfort can be removed through the formation, development and maintenance of the ability to take rapid quality decisions.

Determination

810. Spouses need to protect their children with determination when and as needed.

811. Determination is a quality that helps us and contributes greatly to achieving a happy marriage.

812. Determination is a quality that helps us and contributes greatly to the achievement of our personal goals.

813. Determination is a quality that helps us and contributes greatly to maintaining a happy marriage.

Development

814. The solutions to the problems we have or that we want to solve can be found also through the contribution of the formation, development, maintenance and usage of respectful behavior.

815. Pessimism can be removed and replaced with optimism also through the contribution of the formation, development, maintenance and usage of hardworking behavior.

816. Hopes can be created also through the contribution of the formation, development, maintenance and usage of cheerful behavior.

817. Our own happiness can be achieved and maintained also through the contribution of the formation, development, maintenance

and usage of continuous self perfecting behavior.

818. Our happiness depends a lot also on the formation, development, maintenance and usage of joyful behavior.

819. We can become stronger and we can not allow ourselves to be influenced by the world also through the contribution of the formation, development, maintenance and usage of ingenious behavior.

820. Our future can be projected and achieved also through the contribution of the formation, development, maintenance and usage of idealistic behavior.

821. We can become stronger and we can not allow ourselves to be influenced by the world also through the contribution of the formation, development, maintenance and usage of sturdy behavior.

822. The radical transformation for the better of our life can be achieved also through the formation, development, maintenance and usage of joyful behavior.

823. Some mistakes can be prevented also through the contribution of the formation, development, maintenance and usage of imaginative behavior.

824. The radical transformation for the better of our life can be achieved also through the formation, development, maintenance and usage of leading behavior.

825. Our own happiness can be achieved and maintained also through the contribution of the formation, development, maintenance and usage of charming behavior.

826. Positive experience can be achieved also through the contribution of the formation, development, maintenance and usage of hold behavior.

827. The radical transformation for the better of our life can be achieved also through the formation, development, maintenance and usage of sportive behavior.

828. Our own happiness can be achieved and maintained also through the contribution of the formation, development, maintenance and usage of analytic behavior.

829. We can overcome the difficulties that we must overcome also through the help of the formation, development, maintenance and usage of bold behavior.

830. We can contribute to the achievement of our greatest accomplishments also through the contribution of the formation, development, maintenance and usage of funny behavior.

831. We can form, develop and maintain the state of being ourselves also through the contribution of the formation, development, maintenance and usage of a cheerful behavior.

832. Positive experience can be achieved also through the contribution of the formation, development, maintenance and usage of a behavior with a theoretic spirit.

833. We can form, develop and maintain the state of being ourselves also through the contribution of the formation, development, maintenance and usage of a joyful behavior.

834. We can prevent the falling apart of a happy marriage also through the contribution of the formation, development, maintenance and usage of firm behavior.

835. Our happiness depends a lot also on the formation, development, maintenance and usage of analytic behavior.

836. The obstacles that prevent us from achieving our personal goals can be surpassed also through the contribution of the formation, development, maintenance and usage of spontaneous behavior.

837. Our resistance to changing for the better can be overcome also through the contribution of the formation, development, maintenance and usage of a behavior of being in love with life.

838. Hopes can be created also through the contribution of the formation, development, maintenance and usage of persevering behavior.

839. Problems cannot be solved by the ideas that created them but also through the contribution of the formation, development, maintenance and usage of peaceful behavior.

840. The necessary qualities in achieving personal goals can be formed, developed, maintained and used also through the

contribution of the formation, development, maintenance and usage of sturdy behavior.

841. The radical transformation for the better of our life can be achieved also through the formation, development, maintenance and usage of fighting behavior.

842. Our future can be projected and achieved also through the contribution of the formation, development, maintenance and usage of organized behavior.

843. The limits of achievement imposed by ourselves in our mind at a given moment can be overcome or eliminated also through the contribution of the formation, development, maintenance and usage of balanced behavior.

844. Our happiness depends a lot also on the formation, development, maintenance and usage of balanced behavior.

845. Our happiness depends a lot also on the formation, development, maintenance and usage of adaptable behavior.

846. The necessary qualities in achieving personal goals can be formed, developed,

maintained and used also through the contribution of the formation, development, maintenance and usage of vivacious behavior.

Difficulties

847. Some of those who are very reserved have more difficulties in achieving success in life.

848. People who are not careful with others have more difficulties in maintaining a happy marriage.

849. The uncertainty of incomes sometimes creates difficulties for some marriages and in maintaining a happy marriage.

850. People who are not careful with others have difficulties in achieving a happy marriage.

851. People who are not careful with others have difficulties in achieving mature love.

852. People who are not careful with others have difficulties in finding the right partner for life.

853. People who have had successes also have difficulties.

854. Optimism helps us get through life's difficulties a lot easier.

855. Imagination is a main factor that helps us a lot to face life's difficulties.

856. Ambiguous situations create many difficulties in achieving personal goals.

857. Some ambiguous situations create many difficulties in achieving more and greater successes.

858. True friendships help us in difficult periods of life to face difficulties.

859. People with prejudices have many difficulties because of prejudices to succeed in life.

860. Enthusiastic behavior increases our chances to face life's difficulties.

861. We can overcome the difficulties that we need to overcome also through the formation, development and maintenance of a positive enterprising spirit.

862. We can overcome the difficulties that we need to overcome also through the formation, development and maintenance of quality in everything that we do.

863. We can overcome the difficulties that we need to overcome also through the

formation, development and maintenance of preventive thinking.

864. We can overcome the difficulties that we need to overcome also through the formation, development and maintenance of the sense of fairness in everything we do.

865. People who are not careful with others have difficulties in participating in achieving efficient co operations.

866. The uncertainty of incomes sometimes creates difficulties in achieving a cause.

867. The need to succeed sometimes creates, for some persons, great difficulties in achieving happy marriages.

868. We can overcome difficulties that we must overcome also through the formation, and development and maintenance of efficient thinking.

869. We can overcome difficulties that we must overcome also through the formation, and development and maintenance of the efficient co operations necessary in surpassing the difficulties that we are having.

870. We can overcome difficulties that we must overcome also through the formation, development, maintenance and usage of the sense of self control.

871. In order to change the desire of changing into reality it is necessary to form, develop, maintain and use the ability to know the difficulties that must be overcome.

Diligent

872. The obstacles that prevent us from achieving our personal goals can be surpassed also through the contribution of the formation, development, maintenance and usage of diligent behavior.

873. Positive experience can be achieved also through the contribution of the formation, development, maintenance and usage of diligent behavior.

874. Our resistance to changing for the better can be overcome also through the contribution of the formation, development, maintenance and usage of diligent behavior.

875. Hopes can be created also through the contribution of the formation, development, maintenance and usage of diligent behavior.

876. Some mistakes can be prevented also through the contribution of the formation, development, maintenance and usage of diligent behavior.

877. Release from our self-imposed restrictions can be made also through the contribution of the formation, development, maintenance and usage of diligent behavior.

878. We can contribute to the achievement of our greatest accomplishments also through the contribution of the formation, development, maintenance and usage of diligent behavior.

879. We can prevent the falling apart of a happy marriage also through the contribution of the formation, development, maintenance and usage of diligent behavior.

880. The limits of achievement imposed by ourselves in our mind at a given moment can be overcome or eliminated also through the contribution of the formation, development, maintenance and usage of diligent behavior.

Discipline

881. The indisciplined one is always put first on the list of dismissals.

882. Those who are disciplined have fewer failures.

883. Those who are disciplined are less wrong.

884. The rigorous and disciplined at work have much greater opportunities to obtain and maintain employment. Rigor and discipline at the workplace can be easy if we want to, if we do not have it. Rigor and discipline are two keys to getting a job if you do not have it, or if we have one, they are keys to keeping it. Good luck.

885. The disciplined man is an engine of progress in all the fields of activity.

886. In everything we do we must be disciplined. We know all the rules but unfortunately we do not respect most in many situations

887. He who is disciplined always has a secured job.

888. He who is disciplined is much better than the unruly one.

889. He who is disciplined is appreciated, respected and rewarded.

890. We can make our life more beautiful if we are disciplined.

891. If we are indisciplined we will have many failures in life.

892. In everything we do we need to be disciplined. We all know this but unfortunately many of us do not respect it in many situations.

893. He who is disciplined always has employment.

894. He who is disciplined is much better than the disorderly one.

895. Those who are undisciplined commit many mistakes in their life.

896. A disciplined man has a greater potential to achieve a more beautiful life.

897. A disciplined man has a high potential to achieve a true mature love.

898. A disciplined man more easily and faster achieves efficient co operations.

899. A disciplined man has a greater potential to achieve a happy life.

900. A disciplined man has a greater potential to achieve more and greater outstanding performances.

901. A disciplined man has a great potential to increase his efficiency.

902. Those who are disciplined succeed more easily.

903. Those who are disciplined have more chances to obtain happiness.

904. Those who are disciplined have more chances to achieve efficient co operations.

905. Those who are disciplined have more chances to find their partner for life.

906. Those who are remarkably gifted are disciplined.

907. People who can prevent possible mistakes are disciplined.

908. Problems cannot be solved by the ideas that created them but also through the contribution of the formation, development.

maintenance and usage of Self-imposed disciplined behaviors.

909. Successes are achieved if we are disciplined.

Dynamic

910. Good humor makes us more dynamic.

911. Love is a dynamic process, constantly transforming itself.

912. Those who are very active, dynamic, are more likely to encounter more favorable opportunities.

913. Hopes make us be more dynamic.

914. Luck runs into the one who is active, dynamic and industrious.

915. People who have success have a very dynamic behavior.

Efficient

916. Hiring the best people helps us achieve more efficient co operations.

917. Preventing the inefficient use of human resources helps us achieve more successes.

918. Discovering true instincts helps us achieve more efficient co operations.

919. The art of solving disagreements helps us achieve more efficient co operations.

920. The daily gathering of as much experience as possible helps us achieve more efficient co operations.

921. Preventing negative thinking helps us achieve more efficient co operations.

922. Preventing the inefficient use of material resources helps us achieve more records.

923. The power to continuously efficiently organize things helps us achieve more personal goals.

924. Openness towards new efficient actions helps us achieve more favorable chances.

925. Confidence in the success of what we do helps us achieve more efficient co operations.

926. The art of solving difficult problems helps us achieve more efficient co operations.

927. Learning from the others' mistakes helps us achieve more efficient co operations.

928. The power to continuously efficiently organize things helps us achieve more pleasant surprises.

929. The power of continuous efficient organization helps us achieve much good luck.

930. The daily gathering of as much useful knowledge as possible helps us achieve more efficient co operations.

931. Team spirit helps us achieve more efficient co operations.

932. The desire to be efficient helps us achieve more true friendships.

933. Imitating efficient actions helps us achieve more performances.

934. Openness towards new challenges helps us achieve more efficient co operations.

935. Rising after a failure helps us achieve more efficient co operations.

936. The power of continuous efficient organization helps us achieve more performances.

Efforts

937. Some successes are due only to the qualities and exceptional efforts of people without the participation of any favorable circumstances.

938. Although it is very difficult to maintain a happy marriage it is worth making all the necessary efforts. Continue that you will surely succeed. It is necessary to do it and to persevere. Good luck.

939. There are certain situations for certain persons who do not make excessive efforts and meet favorable situations, which have helped to achieve what they wanted, but they are not at all the same for everyone.

940. Think of yourselves when you do something legal or illegal even if the guilty one can go to prison. You had better pay extra attention; it does not require great efforts and is not worth doing many years in prisons.

941. Achieving a happy marriage is not done by itself, but through many efforts, much dedication, a lot of tolerance, more rational compromises, mutual trust between spouses, a lot of communication, much mutual respect, a lot of knowledge, a lot of wisdom on both sides, much fairness, etc.

942. There are certain situations for certain persons who, without too great efforts, have met with favorable situations which have helped them get what they wanted, but they are not reachable to everybody.

943. Some successes are due only to outstanding efforts and to the people's participation and without any favorable situations

944. Effective state investments in an education that is corresponding and against the disobedience of laws is worth the efforts, because if it is of a good quality, very effective and very attentively created it produces multiple and various effects paying back the positive investments made and an additional huge profit if analyzed in terms of financial efficiency of the investment.

945. Some of us are extremely glad when we manage to achieve a personal goal or more personal goals, and others have consumed their joys during their efforts in their work done to achieve that goal or those goals.

946. The successes we obtain motivate us a lot in the efforts to achieve other successes.

947. Learning and applying strategies of achieving happiness do not require many efforts but many people do almost nothing to learn and apply them although they may help create their own happiness.

948. A happy marriage is achieved through continuous efforts, through searching, finding and applying the necessary knowledge of achievement.

949. The necessary efforts and time needed to achieve a happy marriage must be done and allocated because what a happy marriage can offer us we cannot obtain somewhere else and it is priceless for our good and happiness.

950. The necessary efforts and the time needed to maintain a happy marriage is worth doing and respectively allocating because what a

happy marriage can offer us we cannot obtain somewhere else and it is priceless for our good and happiness.

951. Imagination can be developed with low psychical efforts but with potentially great effects.

952. True friendships are worth the efforts of being achieved.

953. Positive actions surely take us to larger or smaller successes, even if we realize them with bigger or smaller efforts.

Energetic

954. Energetic people have increased chances to achieve a real mature love.

955. Energetic people have more chances of becoming even more efficient.

956. An energetic man has more chances to achieve a more beautiful life.

957. An energetic man has more chances to achieve true love.

958. Energetic men have more chances of achieving their happiness.

959. Energetic men have more chances of achieving more and greater successes.

960. An energetic man has much more chances to achieve a happy marriage.

961. Entertainment makes us more energetic.

962. Energetic people have more chances to meet more favorable situations.

963. An energetic man has much more chances to achieve outstanding performances.

964. Energetic people have much more chances to achieve personal goals.

965. Energetic people have the chances to achieve efficient co operations a lot easier.

966. People who have successes are mostly energetic.

967. A great capacity of having an even more energetic life helps us become more understanding.

968. A great capacity of having an even more energetic life helps us achieve more personal goals.

969. A great capacity of having an even more energetic life helps us maintain our tolerance.

970. A great capacity of having an even more energetic life helps us become more tolerant.

971. The self efficient use of our time helps us become energetic.

972. A great capacity of having an even more energetic life helps us become more optimistic.

973. In order to prevent failures it is necessary to also form, develop, maintain and use energetic behavior.

974. We can prevent some failures also through the contribution of the formation, development, maintenance and usage of energetic behavior.

975. We can become stronger and we can not allow ourselves to be influenced by the world also through the contribution of the formation, development, maintenance and usage of energetic behavior.

976. Creativity helps us become energetic.

977. The force of our ideas can be augmented also through the contribution of the formation, development, maintenance and usage of energetic behavior.

978. The limits of achievement imposed by ourselves in our mind at a given moment can be overcome or eliminated also through the contribution of the formation, development, maintenance and usage of energetic behavior.

979. A great capacity of having an even more energetic life helps us maintain our happiness.

980. Continuous self perfection helps us become energetic.

981. Continuously making ourselves efficient helps us become energetic.

Events

982. The richness of the soul prevents much meanness.

983. The richness of the soul prevents many arguments.

984. Achieving exchanges of information prevents many possible mistakes.

985. A winner's mentality prevents many mistakes.

986. The greater good prevents many conflicts.

987. The sense of responsibility prevents many failures.

988. Balance prevents some possible failures.

989. Entertainment prevents stress.

990. The joy of knowledge prevents stress.

991. The joy of discovery prevents stress.

992. A broad picture creates opportunities of participation in major events.

993. Efficient work prevents poverty.

994. Discipline prevents many unpleasant surprises.

995. Discipline prevents much trouble.

996. Positive ambition prevents many negative facts.

997. Optimistic attitude prevents many failures.

998. Laughter prevents stress.

999. Optimism prevents many failures.

1000. Optimism prevents many troubles.

1001. Skill prevents many mistakes.

1002. The inner beauty of the woman prevents many troubles.

1003. There are events in the history of a love relationship that remain immortal.

1004. The self-control of our flaws prevents many divorces.

1005. The self-control of our flaws prevents many troubles.

1006. Using adverse events in our favor helps us achieve more favorable chances.

1007. Using adverse events in our favor helps us achieve more records.

1008. Using adverse events in our favor helps us achieve more favorable situations.

Evolution

1009. Knowledge, sooner or later, produces revolutionary or smaller changes.

1010. Advances in knowledge and certain new ideas can cause more revolutions in some areas of activity.

1011. The Internet, software and technologies of knowledge produce large revolutions in all areas of activity.

1012. Those who have had better economic and social conditions during their evolution have a higher potential to succeed in life.

1013. Those who have had better social and economic conditions during their evolution have the capacity to maintain social relations.

1014. Those who have had better economic and social conditions during their evolution usually have a higher capacity to achieve a more beautiful life.

1015. Those who have had better economic and social conditions during their evolution have a greater ability to prevent more failures.

1016. Those who have had better economic and social conditions during their evolution usually have a greater ability to achieve a more beautiful life.

1017. Those who have had better economic and social conditions during their evolution have a greater potential to achieve the desired social relations.

1018. Those who have had better economic and social conditions during their evolution have a greater capacity to become even more effective.

1019. Those who have had better economical and social conditions during their evolution have a greater ability to achieve themselves.

1020. Those who have had better economical and social conditions during their evolution achieve the desired efficient co operations.

1021. Those who have had that better economical and social conditions during their evolution have a greater capacity to achieve more and greater successes.

1022. Those who have had better economical and social conditions during their evolution usually have trust in the future.

1023. Those who have had better economical and social conditions during their evolution mostly have the ability to become more efficient.

1024. Those who have had better economical and social conditions during their evolution have the capacity to maintain mature love.

Expand

1025. In life for as long as we live it is necessary, but also madatory that we continually expand our inner potential and this should be a primary and continuous objective.

1026. It is necessary for each of us to have the objective to seek daily methods, solutions so as to continuously expand the efficiency of our time.

1027. Permanently, for as long as we live we need and must be especially wary and continuously expand our capacity of forethought.

1028. Permanently, every day, it is very useful to expand the effectiveness of our self-lesrning.

1029. We continuously expand the effectiveness of positive thinking.

1030. The more we expand the capacity of creation of creative thinking the more the number of ideas and solutions designed to achieve personal goals will increase.

1031. By applying one or more ideas from these books and magazines we expand opportunities for achieving our personal goals.

1032. Many of us still use our time more inefficiently than we can. Each of us has very large reserves and resources to greatly expand the effectiveness of using our time and we should use them to continually expand the efficiency of our time.

1033. In any action we act, we expand its effectiveness if we document everything better.

1034. Effective behaviors help us expand opportunities to achieve positive personal goals.

1035. Psychological balance helps us greatly expand our effectiveness continuously.

1036. Continuously, day by day, we need to expand our capacity to produce as many useful ideas as we can.

1037. The more we expand more effectively our actions the more opportunities we have that we can meet on several favorable occasions.

Expectations

1038. Our objectives create expectations that along with objectives and the actions we do to achieve them make us feel alive.

1039. I have as a personal priority to achieve an increasing number of constructive, effective, harmonious relations, with mutual trust with as many people as possible from all countries to cooperate effectively and support each other in achieving the personal objectives of each of us. Together we acomplish a lot of great deeds. I would be happy for people who read my writings and agree and apply one or more ideas to build as more and more efficient cooperations as they can for each of us and for mankind. The possibilities and potential co operations are endless with me because I have projects in areas which may involve a large number of people. Waiting with confidence and very high expectations for your cooperation with concrete proposals in areas of activity and actions that we want to achieve and any idea, opinion, etc.

1040. Mature love exists due to the relationship between interpersonal love, mutual satisfaction of needs, objectives and personal expectations of the persons involved.

1041. Expectations are creative roads for us.

1042. Expectations make us more confident in ourselves.

Experience

1043. Those who willingly express their positive experience have of greater ability to achieve their desired social relations.

1044. Those who willingly express their positive experience have of greater ability to achieve a motivated life.

1045. Those who willingly express their positive experience continuously increase their ability of becoming more performing.

1046. Our present scientific knowledge, the human experience related to marriage, love can contribute in a short time in the formation and development of a powerful science of forming and maintaining a happy marriage.

1047. Humanist scientific knowledge, human living experience, stored in books, on the Internet, in the media, human qualities allow the achievement of an incredibly high number of happy marriages, but, unfortunately, many people do not give the time and the attention necessary to achieving and maintaining a happy marriage.

1048. Past and present experiences help us make friends.

1049. Past and present experiences contribute a lot in increasing the efficiency of our actions.

1050. The richness of our life experience helps us and increases our chances of achieving a happy marriage.

1051. Those who willingly expand their positive experience must be appreciated.

1052. Past and present experience contributes a lot to preventing many failures.

1053. The richness of our experience helps us a lot to prevent many mistakes.

1054. Experience often brings us luck.

1055. Young people need and must be very careful not to make the same mistakes as their predecessors by taking from their experience only positive models and experience

1056. Self control can be obtained through experiences, through training, through imitation, through study, etc.

1057. Past and present experiences contribute a lot in achieving a more beautiful life.

1058. Our rich life experience helps us achieve a true, mature love.

Facing

1059. In life, it is necessary to allow ourselves to be influenced only by positive influences, and when facing potential negative influences we must be immune.

1060. Those who have the ability of facing mental stress have more chances and a higher potential to achieve their desired future.

1061. A great capacity of facing one's own life helps us become more loved.

1062. A great capacity of facing one's own life helps us become more humane.

1063. A great capacity of facing one's own life helps us become practical.

1064. A great capacity of facing one's own life helps us maintain our tolerance.

1065. A great capacity of facing one's own life helps us achieve more successes.

1066. A great capacity of facing one's own life helps us become more productive.

1067. A great capacity of facing one's own life must be appreciated.

Factors

1068. Successes are also the result of many factors favorable to success.

1069. Success in actions is a result of many factors that are favorable to success.

1070. The more distant the future is the more the factors that will influence it will be more numerous and some more unknown to us.

1071. The life of each of us is influenced by a very large number of factors, which affect us a lot, or less than others or very little. The influence of each factor differs one from the other.

1072. The life of each of us is influenced by us once, that is the by our internal factors, which are very large in number, among which we can remember: 1) our health, 2) our values, 3) our objectives, 4) our qualities 5) our thinking, 6) if we think long term or short-term, or joined, completed, 7) our ability, 8) our gender, 9) our age, etc.

1073. The life each of us is influenced externally or rather by external factors. They can be in a big or small quantity from case to case, from a certain age to another age, etc.. Among them we can enumerate: 1) the school that we attend, 2) people whom come into contact with, 3) the information that we are provided, 4) the Internet, 5) the books we read, study, 6) the environment in which we live 7) the resources at our disposal, 8) the level of development of the society in which we live, etc.

1074. Factors. The influence of external factors on our lives may have greater or less influence over us. This influence can be a positive influence with positive effects on our lives, on our personality development, not a negative influence, with negative effects on our lives, on our personal development.

1075. The continuous return of any harmful behavior for us is one of the factors that make us happy a lot of times.

1076. Establishing concrete, realistic, continuous objectives, immediate or futuristic is also the continuous and effective action to achieve and complete them continuously with other objectives. Needed for their fulfillment are factors that create a lot of happiness, without which we may never get to be happy.

1077. In life we may each receive more or less unjust blows. No unjust blow should consume us, because if we consume ourselves we do not solve anything but instead we harm us and sometimes even very much and we also complicate some problems that we have.

1078. The common values in a marriage are the main factors to maintaining a happy marriage.

1079. We will certainly be better if we act effectively to be better in addition to other factors that make us better.

1080. The more we know about the conditions and factors that contribute to achieving a mature love, the more chances we have to obtain that love.

1081. The causes of bankruptcies of firms are infinite, some can be known and it can be predicted that those company will go bankrupt. Other causes come from externally generated factors incontrollable by us, like the unexpected bankruptcy of some clients and we can not collect money from them anymore, etc.

1082. Successes are achieved by many positive factors.

Facts

1083. Positive facts have multiple positive effects.

1084. Positive facts should be valued.

1085. We could not even imagine many real facts.

1086. While making positive facts we cannot make negative facts.

1087. While we think of positive facts we can no longer think of negative facts.

1088. We must always prevent unsuccessful facts.

1089. Unsuccessful facts should never discourage us.

1090. Our superficiality is a cause of many unsuccessful facts.

1091. Some positive special facts create heroes.

1092. In life it is fair and onest not to make promises that we know we cannot keep, because these facts damage both the one we make them to and ourselves as well.

1093. The enthusiasm of the masses, in some cases, can create some amazing facts.

1094. Not recognizing a man's positive facts damages him.

1095. We need to appreciate and support selfless ideas, to promote, to make them become facts.

1096. Positive facts need to be appreciated.

1097. Those who lack logic in many situations also have many unsuccessful facts.

1098. When you are a novice in an area it is necessary not to give our opinion being ignorant of the facts in that area.

1099. Incredible facts are made mostly by people who have long-term objectives and work with dedication to achieve them.

1100. Usually, only incredible objectives can lead us to incredible facts.

1101. People have already made enormously many facts that were once incredible to achieve.

1102. The facts that are incredible to achieve and that have been achieved show us that many problems that many people still have at the moment can be certainly solved if they believe that they can resolve them if they act with dedication to their resolution.

1103. Our facts of the past, present, or future most influence our future.

1104. Our future is composed of all the facts, feelings, etc. that will be done, that we shall live from now on in our entire life.

1105. Positive deeds create many positive facts.

1106. Preventing negative facts helps us achieve more efficient co operations.

1107. Preventing negative facts helps us achieve much good luck.

1108. Preventing negative facts helps us achieve more records.

1109. Preventing negative facts helps us achieve more personal goals.

Failure

1110. We can prevent failures also through the contribution of the formation, development, maintenance and usage of nondiscriminatory behaviors.

1111. We can prevent failures also through the contribution of the formation, development, maintenance and usage of social behaviors.

1112. We can prevent failures also through the contribution of the formation, development, maintenance and usage of self-control behaviors.

1113. We can prevent failures also through the contribution of the formation, development, maintenance and usage of the ability to efficiently organize our time.

1114. Hesitating behavior is the cause of many failures.

1115. Positive thinking helps us prevent many possible failures.

1116. A positive conception of life helps us a lot to prevent many failures.

1117. A man used to approach problems simultaneously from different points of view has greater chances to prevent more possible failures.

1118. The uncertainty of incomes may make us have more failures.

1119. Our choices influence enormously our success or failure.

1120. Optimistic attitude prevents many failures.

1121. Hopes prevent many failures.

1122. Optimistic women have fewer failures in life.

1123. When spouses are optimistic they have more chances to have fewer failures in life.

1124. Love failures must never discourage us.

1125. Failures in friendships must never discourage us.

1126. Even if we have had many failures in achieving true friendships we must persevere until we succeed.

1127. We must never let ourselves be brought down by failures.

1128. Failures must be used to succeed.

1129. Some failures can contribute enormously to achieving incredible successes.

1130. Failures must never lead us to panic.

1131. Failures can be prevented.

1132. In life, we will succeed if we do not let ourselves be brought down by failures.

1133. Optimism prevents many failures.

1134. Optimism contributes a lot to preventing many failures.

1135. By understanding ourselves we have more chances to prevent more failures.

1136. Knowing ourselves helps us a lot to prevent many failures.

1137. The self-control of our flaws helps us a lot to prevent many failures.

Favorable

1138. Calculated people are more likely to encounter much more favorable circumstances.

1139. Effective co operations increase our chances to meet more favorable circumstances.

1140. Spiritual self-development done continuously, day by day, for as long as we live greatly increases our chances to have more opportunities to meet much more favorable circumstances.

1141. Positive influences help us to greatly increase our chances to meet more favorable situations.

1142. If we have many friends who have had more successes they help us have more chances to meet more favorable situations.

1143. Effective behaviors help us have more chances to meet favorable situations.

1144. Some successes are due mostly to favorable circumstances and a lot less to people.

1145. Some successes are due in a large measure to the quality of people in less favorable situations.

1146. Those who seek favorable situations through perseverance and are better documented will find favorable situations.

1147. Those who did not seek favorable situations say that everything is unfortunate that they are not looking to blame, they are passive and expect luck to come to them from haven.

1148. There are certain situations for certain persons who, without too great efforts, have met with favorable situations which have helped them get what they wanted, but they are not reachable to everybody.

1149. In life we have many more chances to meet favorable situations if we are friends with as many people as we can who have had successes, who have qualities, skills, effective behaviors, creative qualities, which are well documented in areas that concern us all.

1150. Discipline in what we do help us very much to have more chances to meet more favorable situations.

1151. Principles help us have more chances of meeting more favorable situations.

1152. Inadequate education reduces the number and quality of opportunities to find favorable situations.

1153. Responsibility helps us have more chances to meet more favorable situations.

1154. The Internet helps us have more chances to meet much more favorable circumstances.

1155. Only efficient actions help us obtain more favorable opportunities.

1156. Selflessness helps us have more and more chances of meeting favorable situations.

1157. Each of us needs to act continuously against vices because they also reduce our chances of meeting favorable situations.

1158. Fairness helps us have more chances to meet favorable situations.

1159. By more effectively using our time we increase even more our chances of meeting as many favorable situations as we can.

1160. An efficient communication increases our chances of meeting favorable situations.

1161. Wisdom helps us as contributes to obtaining more favorable chances.

1162. The desire to succeed helps us have more chances of meeting favorable situations.

1163. Looking for the necessary knowledge to achieve the objectives continuously increases our chances of meeting favorable situations.

Fear

1164. Fear in a particular area of activity has hindered progress in that area.

1165. Routine is very necessary and useful in behavior, etc. in actions for a certain period of time. After a certain period of time, at a certain time it is necessary to get rid of a certain routine, a certain behavior, a way of thinking, a certain kind of action, etc.. and replace it with another behavior more efficiently, more operational, more tactful, more thoughtful, etc.. in order to progress in achieving what we proposed, our personal objectives. When we need to get rid, to escape a certain routine it is necessary to get rid of it immediately, without doubts, delay, fears, etc. and to act in the new action, new behavior more effectively, without any delay. People who have the ability to leave a certain routine immediately when they need to, progress much faster in life, carry out much faster and more efficient personal goals, performe in live many more bigger or smaller successes than those who do not get rid of a particular or specific routine when necessary. Routine, when we get rid of it when necessary is a big negative factor of progress, it creates many failures, misfortunes, difficulties in achieving personal goals in life, it creates misunderstandings in families and may even lead to divorce, misunderstandings and even conflicts between large generations etc.. The routine of a normal fact, when we can not get rid of it, and it is necessary to get rid of it, it may actually become a very harmful fact for our new family, for the people around, for society, for younger generations and for the future, it may sometimes have many negative effects, very large and very diverse ones. For these reasons it is necessary to continuously develop our ability to get rid of routine when needed immediately.

1166. Fear to act in a certain field is created sometimes by having no experience in that field.

1167. Fear to act in a certain field is created sometimes by the lack of knowledge

1168. Fear stops us from making certain mistakes.

1169. Fear determines us to be more thoughtful.

1170. Fear makes us be more careful.

1171. We must not have exaggerated fears when we start something.

1172. A man with courage participates to efficient global co operations without fear.

1173. Eliminating the fear of failure helps us achieve much good luck.

1174. Eliminating the fear of failure helps us achieve more successes.

1175. Eliminating the fear of failure helps us achieve more favorable chances.

1176. Eliminating the fear of failure helps us achieve more pleasant surprises.

1177. Eliminating the fear of failure helps us achieve more efficient co operations.

1178. Eliminating the fear of failure helps us achieve more true friendships.

1179. Eliminating the fear of failure helps us achieve more favorable situations.

1180. Eliminating the fear of failure helps us achieve more performances.

1181. Eliminating the fear of failure helps us achieve more personal goals.

Flexible

1182. The sense of achieving quality in everything we do inspires us to be more flexible.

1183. Reason helps us be flexible.

1184. Those who are remarkably gifted are flexible.

1185. We can prevent some failures also through the contribution of the formation, development, maintenance and usage of flexible behaviors.

1186. We can form, develop, maintain and use an open mind also through the contribution of the formation, development, maintenance and usage of a flexible behavior.

1187. Prevention can be achieved also through the contribution of the formation, development, maintenance and usage of flexible behaviors.

1188. Stress can be prevented through flexible behaviors.

1189. We can contribute to achieving our happiness by adopting flexible behaviors.

1190. True mature love makes lovers be more flexible with each other.

1191. Love sometimes makes us more flexible.

1192. Our chances of becoming happy increase if we are flexible.

1193. In order to follow and transform our personal goals into reality, it is necessary to also form, develop, maintain and use our flexible behavior.

1194. The necessary qualities in achieving personal goals can be formed, developed, maintained and used also through the contribution of the formation, development, maintenance and usage of flexible behavior.

1195. A great capacity of being flexible helps us become more preventive.

1196. A great capacity of being flexible helps us become more efficient.

1197. A great capacity of being flexible helps us become happy.

1198. Continuously making ourselves efficient helps us become flexible.

1199. Some mistakes can be prevented also through the contribution of the formation, development, maintenance and usage of flexible behavior.

1200. A great capacity of being flexible helps us maintain our way of being cautious.

1201. A great capacity of being flexible helps us achieve more successes.

Focus

1202. We can encounter more easily favorable situations for us if we continue to focus on our activities.

1203. To achieve quality actions to become happy and maintain our happiness, it is necessary that every time we act to focus totally on that action, to be careful in everything we do. Any little distraction can have grater or smaller negative effects on our happiness. Because of this, our happiness totally depends on our overall happiness and on the quality of actions which we achieve, on the concentration and attention with which we perform them.

1204. In life we may each receive more or less unjust blows. No unjust blow should consume us, because if we consume ourselves we do not solve anything but instead we harm us and sometimes even very much and we also complicate some problems that we have.

1205. First of all when we receive an unjust blow, we should focus on finding solutions, actions to help us minimize the negative effects of the blow, unless we can reduce them to zero.

1206. Secondly, it is necessary to identify the causes and factors that led us to receiving them unjustly.

1207. Thirdly, it is necessary to remove the causes that led us to receiving them unjustly, so that we shall not receive them again or several times again.

1208. In the fourth line is necessary to take all necessary measures to prevent the causes that led us to reciving the X blow unjustly.

1209. Fifthly it is necessary to seek to identify whether there are other causes that might lead us to receive further blows unjustly.

1210. Sixthly it is necessary to discover other potential causes that could cause us to receive more unfair blows by taking the necessary measures: 1) to eliminate these causes, 2) where we can not prevent these causes it is necessary to take the necessary measures not to receive them unjustly, 3) if we receive them, to make the blow have as little negative effects as possible over us.

1211. In the seventh line it is necessary that our new situation caused by the unfair blow is used efficiently for us. It is possible that what we accomplish after the new situation created by the unjustly received blow is much larger and beneficial to us than the achievements that we had done if we had not received the blow unjustly.

1212. Increasing the ability to focus our attention helps contribute to the increasing of our efficiency in what we do.

1213. Increasing the ability to focus attention helps us and contributes to achieving independence.

1214. The increased ability to focus our attention helps us contribute greatly to achieving more fulfillments.

1215. Increasing the ability to focus our attention helps us maintain a happy marriage.

1216. A nervous state reduces a lot our capacity to focus.

1217. When we focus on what we are doing we increase our chances to prevent mistakes.

1218. Focusing on what we do is a necessity.

1219. Focusing on what we do helps us a lot to achieve personal goals.

1220. Focusing on what we do helps us make the things we do of good quality.

1221. Focusing on what we do helps us a lot to have even more chances to meet more favorable situations.

1222. The state of restlessness reduces a lot our ability to focus.

1223. In order to pursue and transform our personal goals into reality we need to form, develop, maintain and use the ability to focus.

1224. Keeping the focus on achieving personal goals helps us achieve more true friendships.

1225. Keeping the focus on achieving personal goals helps us achieve more personal goals.

1226. Keeping the focus on achieving personal goals helps us achieve more records.

1227. Keeping the focus on achieving personal goals helps us achieve more favorable situations.

Forces

1. Our successes increase our strength, our confidence in our own forces and the accomplishment of other successes.

2. It is necessary to immediately and continuously join our forces, to be in solidarity to combat all forms of discrimination and to prevent them.

3. It is much more effective, humane, legal, responsible, necessary and required for society to prevent the causes leading to situations in which some people have the need for human protection and to ensure the human protection of people who need it rather than: 1) build prisons, 2) increase the number of police, gendarmerie and other repressive forces. 3) spend large sums on various formal activities of the state's institutions without any actual positive finality, etc.

4. For those who have succeeded in life, who had one or more major successes, the effort they have made to pursue them without problems, to be consumed without having to make big efforts, they made such efforts on their own initiative, without them, someone would do them with great pleasure, without any stress, but it is considered that to succeed it is necessary to make those efforts, those actions. Although efforts, actions were very high, with huge consumption of mental and physical energy, more or less risks they felt of course, normal in order to achieve success, and what they proposed, and this is not to look at the facts not stressed, but on the contrary it has created a state of normality and even additional motivation and desire to do what they have proposed. These ones in contrast with others that the risky, unpredictable, great efforts chased, tried to solve, or attempted to carry out the enormous stress and had much inefficient behavior, but they always made them smarter, more effective, more operational, more powerful, more confident in their forces, in their success, in their future, etc

5. Confidence in our own forces is a creative attitude that helps us and contributes greatly to achieve our personal goals.

6. A person who has no creative attitude, confidence in his own forces, he can auto-shape it, develop and maintain it for life.

7. Confidence in us, in our forces helps in maintaining true friends.

8. Our confidence in our forces makes us be enthusiastic in implementing what we proposed.

9. Confidence in ourselves, in our forces helps us be optimistic.

10. Confidence in ourselves, in our forces, helps and contributes to maintaining a happy marriage.

11. Trust in ourselves, in our forces helps us and contributes to the maintenance of true friends.

12. Presently, mankind wastes its resources for negative activities such as: producing cigarettes, producing arms that exceed the necessary of solving problems in a peaceful way, maintaining overpopulated armies,

maintaining repressive forces used exaggeratedly, etc.

13. Long term thinking develops our trust in our own forces.

14. It is necessary and imperative that each of us, regardless of what country we are from, to have the personal goal of acting with greater efficiency continuously, every day, for as long as we live, for us all to join forces in order to establish normality where there is abnormal as soon as possible and to prevent the establishment of abnormality instead of normality.

15. Successes increase our confidence in ourselves, in our forces.

16. Many of us can perform incredible deeds but we do not, not because we do not have the knowledge and qualities necessary to do them, but because we do not trust ourselves, our forces and some of us because we are not sufficiently motivated.

17. When we trust ourselves and our forces we feel happy.

18. If we are stressed and we get rid of stress, we become more confident in ourselves and in our forces.

19. The desire to succeed many times contributes to achieving many positive forces.

20. Solving problems through positive methods contributes to increasing our trust in our own forces.

Further

1228. In life we may each receive more or less unjust blows. No unjust blow should consume us, because if we consume ourselves we do not solve anything but instead we harm us and sometimes even very much and we also complicate some problems that we have.

1229. First of all when we receive an unjust blow, we should focus on finding solutions, actions to help us minimize the negative effects of the blow, unless we can reduce them to zero.

1230. Secondly, it is necessary to identify the causes and factors that led us to receiving them unjustly.

1231. Thirdly, it is necessary to remove the causes that led us to receiving them unjustly, so that we shall not receive them again or several times again.

1232. In the fourth line is necessary to take all necessary measures to prevent the causes that led us to reciving the X blow unjustly.

1233. Fifthly it is necessary to seek to identify whether there are other causes that might lead us to receive further blows unjustly.

1234. Sixthly it is necessary to discover other potential causes that could cause us to receive more unfair blows by taking the necessary measures: 1) to eliminate these causes, 2) where we can not prevent these causes it is necessary to take the necessary measures not to receive them unjustly, 3) if we receive them, to make the blow have as little negative effects as possible over us.

1235. In the seventh line it is necessary that our new situation caused by the unfair blow is used efficiently for us. It is possible that what we accomplish after the new situation created by the unjustly received blow is much larger and beneficial to us than the achievements that we had done if we had not received the blow unjustly.

1236. We are very harmful in our struggle to become as rich as others. We need and must develop our positive parse, to fill the other etc. so that we can get much further than if we try to become another person.

1237. The disparagement aggression of a member by another family member by society contributes greatly to preventing further aggression among the families and other families, society.

1238. Self-perfecting further increases our chances to find the right partner for life.

1239. We are very harmful in our struggle to become the same as other persons. We are who we are and it is necessary and required for us to develop our positive parts, to complete them with others, etc., so that we get much further than if we tried to become another person.

1240. A man with an orientation towards a further future has greater and more chances to achieve more true friendships.

Future

1241. Periodic analysis of our actions is very necessary to help us increase the effectiveness of future actions.

1242. When the future seems desperate it is necessary to study books on positive thinking.

1243. When the future seems desperate it is necessary to have relationships with successful people.

1244. Wisdom is a resource to our future wealth.

1245. Young people need to be very much involved in creating their future and that of the state they live in.

1246. Young people have the right and obligation to participate as much as possible in creating their future and present of the state they live in, but also of the world.

1247. It is necessary and required of young people, for their good, happiness and future to establish and develop as many and as much powerful non-profit organizations, trade unions, political parties, institutions, legal entities, etc..as they can through which to promote their values, to contribute to their future, to promote and defend their present and future.

1248. It is necessary and obligatory for the young, for their happiness and their future, to act as one to be elected as many as they can in local, municipal, town, county councils, parliaments in countries, such as mayors of villages, towns and other institutions for which elections are made.

1249. Young people from all of the world's states should not be negligent, careless, passive, inactive, non participative in taking decisions that concern them, their present and future, but to take part in decision-making in local councils, central parliaments, governments and other state and non-state institutions, and use all their capacities, abilities, skills, attitudes, knowledge, energy, commitment and desire to assert and achieve great deeds, to create a more humane, more righteous, more happy, with less trouble world.

1250. Our personal goals give us confidence in the future

1251. When we have realistic goals that we believe in and act with dedication to achieve them, we are confident in our future.

1252. The actions of our past, present and future affect the most the quality of our life.

1253. The actions of our past, present and future affect and will affect the quality of our objectives.

1254. Those who do not have realistic objectives to believe in and act with dedication to achieve them, they do not believe in the future.

1255. Most of us think about the future, our future, the future of our children, the future of our loved ones, the future of our country, the future of the world, of what it will be like in the future and how it will be.

1256. Happiness depends on each of us knowing how to choose, preparing and carring out the objectives for the future.

1257. The longer we are able to choose, prepare and carry out projects and objectives for the future, the more realistic the chances are of building a happy future.

1258. Our future depends mostly on us.

1259. The happiness of our future depends mostly on us.

1260. Our facts of the past, present, or future most influence our future.

1261. We can easily achieve outstanding deeds in the future if we choose, project them from now on and persevere to achieve them.

1262. We can learn from the others' positive effective behaviors free of charge, by observing their positive, effective, human behavior. Many of the behaviors that we learn by observation can help us greatly to increase the efficiency of the use of our time, to increase the efficiency of our actions, to achieve faster objectives of our present and future.

1263. Each of us can become wiser freely without offering something in exchange to others every day, if we reflect, every day, on everything that can help us achieve better, faster, all our present and future objectives.

1264. Patience and the art of behaving patiently help us enormously hard to achieve personal present, future goals and ones for the future.

1265. Each of us with the help of the qualities that we have with that of those that we can shape and develop, of the various resources around the world, of the human experience and knowledge acquired in books, on the Internet, in publications, etc. we can be optimistic in our future in achieving a happy future. It is necessary to mobilize the will, qualities given to us with all our being to achieve the personal goal of making a happier future for us. Good luck to all. The ideas exposed by me can help very much, use them.

1266. Often mistakes can teach us a lot if we want to learn from them and to prevent other future mistakes.

1267. People who are always concerned about the future also have creative qualities.

1268. As we have more experience which helps us achieve personal goals all the more confidence we will have in a better future.

1269. Young people must unite for the achievment of a better possible future.

1270. People who are confident in others have faith in the global positive future.

1271. People with an innovative spirit have much greater chances to achieve a positive future.

1272. The man oriented towards a very remote future has more and much greater chances to achieve a beautiful life for himself.

1273. The sense of organization contributes to increasing our trust in the future.

1274. Those who follow their vocation have greater chances to achieve their desired future.

1275. He who is very reserved achieves his desired future much harder.

1276. Those with greater resistance to stress have a higher chance to achieve their desired future.

1277. My mediatations are for our future.

1278. Our orientation towards a very distant future is a creative attitude that helps us a lot to achieve our personal goals.

1279. A person who has no creative attitude oriented towards the future can auto-shape, develop and maintain it for as long as he lives. Good luck.

1280. The creative attitude oriented towards the future helps us very much to resolve more problems more quickly.

1281. Co-development gives us greater confidence in the future.

1282. Often, if we had failures, we can learn much more from them than from successes, but this should not justify our failures, but look for the causes of failures and take preventive measures to stop our future failures.

1283. To make us more easily and quickly achieve our personal goals is to accumulate as much knowledge as possible about how to build the future in what concerns our personal goals.

1284. Our future is very much influenced by our hopes.

1285. The quality of our objectives determines the quality of our future.

1286. The Internet can help us enormously to achieve a happier future.

1287. The actions of our past help us very much to expand the effectiveness of our present and future.

1288. Co-development increases our confidence in the future.

1289. Co- development gives us greater confidence in the future.

1290. Hopes make us more confident in the future.

1291. Experience and useful knowledge that help us obtain personal objectives give us trust in a better future.

1292. Harmonious global co-development thinking makes us more confident in the future.

1293. The more qualities we have to use in achieving personal objectives the more trust we have in a better future.

1294. Those who solve problems only through constructive methods develop their trust in the future.

1295. A positive conception of life contributes a lot in achieving the desired future.

1296. Constructive thinking helps us a lot to achieve our desired future.

1297. The sense of fairness develops our trust in the future.

1298. The sense of commitment in work develops our trust in the future.

1299. Favorable situations help us a lot to achieve our desired future.

1300. Our own value system must contribute to developing our trust in the future.

1301. The state of anger makes it very hard for us to achieve our desired future.

1302. Constructive thinking contributes a lot in achieving a positive global future.

1303. Humanist ideas in the near or far future will create many workplaces in all states of the world.

Goals

1304. By acting continuously and effectively to achieve positive goals we will surely achieve them.

1305. Those who have a preventive thinking have more chances to realize their personal goals than those who do not have a preventive thinking.

1306. Those who act with the greatest devotion to achieve their personal goals, will achieve them much faster, more certainly and at a much higher percentage than those who do not act with the same maximum devotion.

1307. To have the least possible failures in life is we need conversant as necessary to achieve personal goals, without having failures, in order to achieve them.

1308. The documentation necessary to achieve the personal goals we need, we can complete from existing books or with the help of the Internet, in a very effective, cheap and operative way, etc..

1309. Young people from many countries of the world by filling seats that they can in local councils, central ones, in the parliament, government and other institutions and by maximizing the use of the resources available (energy, enthusiasm, optimism, devotion, capacities, values, skills, abilities, knowledge, etc.) can contribute enormously much to accelerating the solving of many problems of their regims, of their goals, and of the world.

1310. Most of us use our time as efficiently as we could. For this reason, through a more efficient use of our time we can achieve much easier our personal goals.

1311. Increasing the quality of each of our actions help us greatly in achieving personal goals.

1312. Skills help us more easily achieve personal goals.

1313. As we develop more skills, the more and bigger chances we have to achieve personal goals. So, it is worth and it is necessary to develop and shape all the skills that we need in order to achieve personal goals.

1314. Through organized, efficient and continuous work, we can solve a lot faster much more personal goals.

1315. Applying in practice many ideas from these books, magazines, etc. you will be able to achieve much easier, much faster and even more personal goals.

1316. The better we know ourselves, the more chances we have to relaunch our personal goals.

1317. Flexibility in thinking and behavior helps us achieve much easier, much faster and a larger number of personal goals.

1318. Flexibility in thinking and behaviors is a quality necessary to achieve personal goals.

1319. Only by making a correct hierarchy, all the time, of our personal goals, according to importance and urgency, we can achieve more personal goals.

1320. The efficient organization of our personal time, continuously, day by day, helps us enormously to achieve our personal goals.

1321. Personal self-motivation is a personal goal, which helps us every day, in achieving other personal goals.

1322. Continuous, day by day, self-progress, helps us very much to achieve other personal goals.

1323. Spiritual self-development, continuous, day by day, helps us contribute enormously to achieving other personal goals.

1324. In life it is necessary to self-impose voluntarily and not obliged by anyone our personal humane goals.

Guide

1325. Positive thinking guides us to success.

1326. Most of those who have not succeeded in creating a happy marriage up to a certain date, in order to succeed they need to form and develop a good self guide to achieve a happy marriage.

1327. Obtaining as many and great successes that we can, can be achieved through the contribution of formation, development, maintenance and usage of the ability to form, develop, maintain and use a proper personal guide to achieve our personal objectives.

1328. Obtaining as many and greatest successes as we can, can be achieved through the formation, development, maintenance and usage of the ability to form, develop, maintain and use a proper personal guide to achieve personal objectives.

Happening

1329. Forming the wrong ideas about what is happening to us can be prevented through the contribution of the formation, development, maintenance and usage of realistic life conceptions.

1330. Forming wrong ideas about what is happening to us can be prevented also through the contribution of the formation, development, maintenance and usage of preventive thinking.

1331. Forming wrong ideas about what is happening to us can be prevented also through the contribution of the formation, development, maintenance and usage of efficient thinking.

1332. Forming wrong ideas about what is happening to us can be prevented also through the contribution of the formation, development, maintenance and usage of an objective conception of life.

1333. Forming the wrong ideas about what is happening to us can be prevented also through the formation, development, maintenance and usage of an optimistic conception of life.

1334. Forming the wrong ideas about what is happening to us can be prevented also through the contribution of the formation, development, maintenance and usage of correct thinking.

1335. Forming wrong ideas about what is happening to us can be prevented also through the contribution of the formation, development, maintenance and usage of a positive conception of life.

1336. Forming wrong ideas about what is happening to us can be prevented also through the contribution of the formation, development, maintenance and usage of a domestic thinking.

1337. Forming wrong ideas about what is happening to us can be prevented also through the formation, development, maintenance and usage of a realistic life conception.

1338. Forming wrong ideas about what is happening to us can be prevented by using a constructive thinking.

1339. Forming wrong ideas about what is happening to us can be achieved also through the contribution of the formation, maintenance and usage of a scientific life conception.

Hardworking

1340. I write to be useful and practical. He who writes every day to as many people as possible, helps them in one way or another, but as much as possible to help them achieve personal goals, brave performances, with strong will, with perseverance, to get as much satisfaction, joy and happiness as they can, to develop a harmonious personality, to be part of as much love for as long as they live, a happy family with happy children, to be hardworking, wise, to have harmony in the family, to have as many relations of friendship and cooperation as they can, to be what makes them better for their family, children and others.

1341. We can create a more beautiful life if we are hardworking.

1342. Sometimes life offers us incredible situations. Some employees are very hardworking, they risk their health and even their life at work for a business to be effective and to succeed and all these employees sometimes steal from the company where they work, harming themselves a lot.

1343. The force of our ideas can be augmented also through the contribution of the formation, development, maintenance and usage of hardworking behavior.

1344. In order to prevent failures it is necessary to also form, develop, maintain and use hardworking behavior.

1345. We can form, develop and maintain the state of being ourselves also through the contribution of the formation, development, maintenance and usage of a hardworking behavior.

1346. Our happiness depends a lot also on the formation, development, maintenance and usage of hardworking behavior.

1347. In order to rise up once again for the first time for the who knows what time it is necessary to also form, develop, maintain and use hardworking behavior.

1348. The radical transformation for the better of our life can be achieved also through the formation, development, maintenance and usage of hardworking behavior.

1349. Rather than lamenting that we do not have successes it is more useful to also form, develop, maintain and use hardworking behavior.

1350. Our future can be projected and achieved also through the contribution of the formation, development, maintenance and usage of hardworking behavior.

1351. Stress can be prevented also through the formation, development, maintenance and usage of hardworking behavior.

1352. We can prevent some failures also through the contribution of the formation, development, maintenance and usage of hardworking behavior.

1353. Aspiring towards a more meaningful life can also be achieved through the formation, development, maintenance and usage of hardworking behavior.

1354. Problems cannot be solved by the ideas that created them but also through the contribution of the formation, development, maintenance and usage of hardworking behavior.

Hesitating

1355. Hesitating behavior reduces the operability of the decisions that we take.

1356. Hesitating behavior makes it very hard for us to achieve our personal goals.

1357. Hesitating behavior reduces our chances of achieving more successes a lot.

1358. Hesitating behavior is harmful for the achievement of efficient co operations.

1359. Hesitating behavior reduces our chances to meet more favorable situations.

1360. Hesitating behavior reduces the chances of achieving efficient co-developments.

1361. Hesitating behavior makes many people not trust us.

1362. Hesitating behavior is the cause of many failures.

1354. Problems cannot be solved by the ideas that created them but also through the contribution of the formation, development, maintenance and usage of hardworking behavior.

Hesitating

1355. Hesitating behavior reduces the operability of the decisions that we take.

1356. Hesitating behavior makes it very hard for us to achieve our personal goals.

1357. Hesitating behavior reduces our chances of achieving more successes a lot.

1358. Hesitating behavior is harmful for the achievement of efficient co operations.

1359. Hesitating behavior reduces our chances to meet more favorable situations.

1360. Hesitating behavior reduces the chances of achieving efficient co-developments.

1361. Hesitating behavior makes many people not trust us.

1362. Hesitating behavior is the cause of many failures.

reliable to obtain more and higher successes.

1369. Sociable people are very open and have much higher chances to achieve personal goals.

1370. Receptive people have much higher chances to maintain a happy marriage.

1371. The man who is understanding has much more are much higher chances to achieve a happy marriage.

1372. The man full of life has much higher and more chances and a greater potential to maintain a happy marriage.

1373. Very sociable people have a higher resistance to stress.

1374. Those with greater resistance to stress have a higher chance to achieve their desired future.

1375. The more efficient use of our time greatly increases our chances to achieve more and higher successes.

1376. Those who are emotionally balanced have a higher potential and greater chance of achieving more and greater successes.

Hopeful

1377. In order to rise up once again for the first time for the who knows what time it is necessary to also form, develop, maintain and use hopeful behavior.

1378. Obtaining more and greater successes can be achieved also through the contribution of the formation, development, maintenance, usage of a hopeful behavior.

1379. Rather than lamenting that we do not have successes it is more useful to also form, develop, maintain and use hopeful behavior.

1380. In order to escape poverty it is necessary to also form, develop, maintain and use hopeful behavior.

1381. We can form, develop and maintain the state of being ourselves also through the contribution of the formation, development, maintenance and usage of a hopeful behavior.

1382. Continuously making ourselves efficient helps us become hopeful.

1383. In order to prevent failures it is necessary to also form, develop, maintain and use hopeful behavior.

1384. Stress can be prevented also through the formation, development, maintenance and usage of hopeful behavior.

Ideal

1385. The size of our life is made up of several parts of what it is necessary to know very well in order to achieve each of them. It is not easy but not impossible. First we must know very clearly, concretely that we want to achieve each of them, when, how, we want to achieve them, etc.. Among them we mention privacy that includes our family life, human relations with friends, our intimate life, our feelings and our thoughts, our intimate writings, journals, autobiographies, blogs, web pages etc. To succeed in this life it is necessary to respect, know the rules of success in this private life. Then there is employment, which includes ideas, thoughts, actions, objectives and professional projects. And here in employment we can succeed only if we respect the rules needed to succeed in our careers. Good behavior is ideal when we can do that to support our private life as much as possible, employment contributes as much as possible to achieve a harmonious private life, with successful private joys, a lot of satisfactions and happiness. If we propose to realize these needs we will establish that we are able to achive personal objectives and performance, great successes, and we will have joys, happiness and satisfactions in life, both in our private and professional one.

Unfortunately, there are still few people who do what they should not do to have failures in both private and professional lives, or in one of them. The most happy and satisfying are called those who made the necessary efforts and who have managed to achieve harmonious, happy privacy, with joys and satisfactions and who have achieved personal goals and projects in employment. From them we can learn many effective models of action, positive behaviors, which will help us achieve our privacy and professionalism.

1386. The Internet is the ideal means to develop as many human relationships as possible.

1387. The more we meet more men or women the better chances we have to meet the right partner for life. An ideal place to meet them is the Internet being aware of the advantages, disadvantages and risks that it offers. Good luck! Persevere because I am sure you will be able to find the right partner for life. Good luck.

1388. Mature love provides the ideal environment for children in a family.

1389. The Internet is an ideal place to facilitate communication and human contact 24 hours a day and it is the most convenient, less costly at any time of day and night way, with a great number of people. Connect to the Internet if you have not connected yet because it is worth doing it. Good luck.

1390. The Internet is ideal as it facilitates and enhances human communication 24 hours a day any day and with the most convenient, low cost at any time of day and night, with an unlimited number of people. Connect to the Internet if you have not signed in yet, because it is worth it. Good luck.

1391. The more men or women we meet from case to case, the better chances we have to meet the right life partner. An ideal place to meet him/her is the Internet, taking into account the advantages, disadvantages and risks that it offers us. Good luck. Persevere as I am sure you will be able to find the right partner for life. Good luck.

Imagination

1392. Our transformation for the better can be achieved also through the contribution of formation, development, maintenance and usage of our imagination.

1393. Imagination can be developed through a broad picture.

1394. Imagination can be formed, developed and maintained by using creative thoughts.

1395. Scientific thinking develops our imagination.

1396. Today's imagination can help us achieve tomorrow's reality.

1397. Today's imagination is a part of tomorrow's reality.

1398. Imagination can be formed.

1399. Imagination can be developed.

1400. Positive imagination increases our chances to achieve more successes.

1401. A positive imagination helps us a lot to achieve our personal goals.

1402. Imagination is an important factor of achieving records.

1403. Imagination must be rewarded.

1404. Imagination must be supported.

1405. Imagination must be appreciated.

1406. Imagination must be impelled.

1407. Positive imagination precedes what lies in the future.

1408. Positive imagination helps us achieve our own happiness.

1409. Positive imagination helps us prevent many conflicts.

1410. Positive imagination helps us prevent many difficulties.

1411. Positive imagination can help us achieve more therefore we can believe that we are able to achieve more.

1412. We must permanently develop our imagination.

1413. Imagination can be developed with low psychical efforts but with potentially great effects.

1414. The time used to developing positive imagination gives special results that are useful to us.

1415. Imagination can contribute to achieving a happy marriage.

1416. Positive imagination can enormously contribute to achieving many performances.

1417. Imagination can help us achieve many special friendships.

1418. Positive imagination can help us achieve many efficient co operations.

1419. Positive imagination can help us find the right pair.

1420. Positive imagination can help us a lot to achieve true love.

1421. Positive imagination can help us a lot to maintain true love.

Importance

1422. The world does not provide the conditions necessary and mandatory for the activities necessary to achieve a performance in raising children and its importance.

1423. Husbands should never forget the importance of sex in maintaining a happy marriage.

1424. The objective of personal planning for our actions continuously, day by day, for as long as we live, contributes greatly to achieving our other goals. It deserves to get our attention because of its importance. Good luck.

1425. The personal goal of effectively organizing our actions continuously, day by day, for as long as we live, contributes greatly to achieving other of our personal objectives. It deserves to receive the necessary attention, because of its importance. Good luck.

1426. Increasing the efficiency of justice should be one of the main objectives of each state, because it is of little importance in many states.

1427. The work of journalists should be more supported by the society, the state and the people, because of its special importance to the good of the people.

1428. The economy of knowledge will be an integral part of maximum importance in humanist economy.

1429. Unfortunately enormously many people do not to give the importance, the attention or the time needed for a true marriage.

1430. The force of our words can be increased through the importance of the message we transmit.

1431. The force of our words can be augmented through the importance of the message we transmit.

Important

1432. Very often, we deal with many issues of lesser importance, of lesser urgency instead of more important and urgent problems.

1433. Each of us has the chance to assert oneself in real life. It is important to discover the chances and to achieve the goal.

1434. Each of us has many potential opportunities to assert themselves in life, it is important to discover and to achieve them.

1435. The science of personal goals should be studied in schools and universities, etc., because it is very important for us to achieve a quality life.

1436. Unfortunately, neither people nor society address the future, are not concerned with the future that is so important to us, with how much it influences our future happiness.

1437. The woman's need for security is very important to her and she tries to satisfy it by marring.

1438. The more effective use of our time should be a priority objective for us, urgent and important for as long as we live, because it is very important in achieving all the objectives of our present and future.

1439. The world' countries need and must take the necessary steps to create and develop every citizen's ability and creative thinking, because they are particularly important for each country and human in part, for the country's problems, the world's problems and the objectives of each man.

1440. Each of us has many chances to assert themselves in life. It is important to seek them, to find them and to work to make them become realities, successes.

1441. In the development of our personality an important role may be played by the help in multiple forms, of family, friends, colleagues from school, work, neighbors, all of which are related.

1442. The bar's activity is extremely important for society, but unfortunately, in many cases, incredibly, it does not have the quality that it should have in almost all the world.

1443. Appropriate effective education that meets human needs and the needs of society is very important both for people and for society, but, unfortunately, even in 2007, many states do not have an effective education that meets the appropriate requirements and education needs of people and society.

1444. The quality of friendships is more important than the quantity of friends.

Improve

1445. The science of preventing human errors should accelerate improvements in the quality of life of people around the globe.

1446. Employers should be supported, encouraged by states to develop their business, to improve, in order to give adequate salaries.

1447. Employers should be supported, encouraged by states to develop a business, to improve it in order to give proper wages.

Increasing

1448. Good morale helps us very much to achieve an increasing efficiency.

1449. Global humanist co operations contribute greatly to increasing opportunities to find more favorable situations.

1450. People who are resistant to stress have more chances to contribute to increasing the efficiency of the group they are in.

1451. The man who operates continuously, day by day, to become more organized has increasing chances to create a happy life.

1452. The sense of organization contributes to increasing our trust in the future.

1453. Love carries each of the parteners step by step through deepening mutual awareness, through the multitude of interrelations, through the needs to support the relationship in achieving personal goals, increasing confidence in one another, etc.

1454. Thinking long term helps us and contributes greatly to increasing our confidence in ourselves.

1455. Increasing the ability to focus our attention helps contribute to the increasing of our efficiency in what we do.

1456. Increasing the motivation we increase our performance.

1457. Increasing the ability to produce as many useful ideas as we can, continually, day by day, for as long as we live should be one of our personal goals.

1458. Increasing the efficiency of justice should be one of the main objectives of each state, because it is of little importance in many states.

1459. Increasing the ability to focus attention helps us and contributes to achieving independence.

1460. Constructive thinking helps us and contributes greatly to the increasing number of opportunities to meet more favorable circumstances.

1461. Promptness helps and contributes to increasing our credibility.

1462. Positive ideas help and contribute to increasing our efficiency.

1463. Increasing the ability to focus our attention helps us maintain a happy marriage.

1464. Those who are mentally self-developed continuously every day, for as long as we live, have increasing opportunities to realize their objectives.

1465. Those who are mentally self-developed continuously every day, for as long as we live, have increasing opportunities to achieve more successes.

1466. Thinking long-term helps and contributes greatly to increasing our confidence in us.

Indecision

1467. Indecision is the cause of many failures.

1468. Indecision is the cause of many accidents.

1469. Indecision is the cause of many casualties.

1470. When we are doubtful we must find solutions to get rid of indecision.

1471. Indecision can sometimes harm us very much.

Inefficient

1472. Those who are slaves to routine life and have many smaller or very big failures, usually small achievements and successes, personal and professional unfulfillments, they are in fact slaves of their own inefficient, clumsy behaviors which affect their efficiency, their quality of the future etc..

1473. The actions of prevention help to prevent many inefficient operations.

1474. Measures to prevent crime do not only reduce prison terms and large punishments with imprisonment, there are much more effective measures from all points of view including a citizen who spends large amounts of money because of the inefficient legal system based only on prison terms.

1475. Not even in 2007 the majority of states do not apply the most effective measures to prevent crime, unfortunately, but apply only primitive and inefficient methods of punishment through prison.

1476. Usually very many of us use our time more inefficiently than we can.

1477. Those who know and have the power to change inefficient behaviors when it is necessary have greater chances to achieve efficient co operations.

1478. Preventive actions help us to prevent a lot more inefficient actions.

1479. If we are inefficient we will have many failures.

1480. If we change, our ideas can become inappropriate and inefficient.

1481. Inefficient behaviors surely lead us to failures.

1482. Shallow inefficient behaviors must be terminated immediately and replaced with effective behaviors.

1483. Inefficient behaviors put barriers in achieving our positive personal goals.

1484. The actions of prevention help and contribute to the prevention of inefficient cooperation.

1485. State institutions unfortunately still have many inefficient regulations that reduce a lot of the possible efficiency to protect the interests of their employees.

1486. Often, unfortunately, we make many inefficient operations that make us sick because of an idea or more belonging to us. So pay attention to the ideas you have.

1487. Inefficient behaviors surely lead us to failure.

1488. Inefficient behaviors should be stopped immediately and replaced with effective behaviors.

1489. Inefficient behaviors prevent us from achieving our positive personal objectives.

Influences

1490. In life, it is necessary to allow ourselves to be influenced only by positive influences, and when facing potential negative influences we must be immune.

1491. Our life is influenced by a very large number of influences.

1492. The quality of our lives can be mostly influenced by us, using in our favor the influences that may affect more or less the quality of life.

1493. Along with many potential influences on our future, if we propose and act, we can mostly influence our future. Depends on how much and how we want to influence it; it depends on how much we let others influence our future.

1494. Unfortunately, neither people nor society address the future, are not concerned with the future that is so important to us, with how much it influences our future happiness.

1495. Many women have had very high positive influences on men, and have helped them achieve outstanding performances.

1496. The man who is conscientious to positive influences achieves others in his life.

1497. To succeed in life it is necessary to guard ourselves against negative influences.

1498. To succeed in life it is necessary continuously, every day, for as long as we live, to have the personal goal to guard ourselves against negative influences.

1499. You must take the necessary measures so that children can not be influenced by negative influences.

1500. If we let ourselves be influenced by negative influences, we have a lot to lose.

1501. If we let ourselves be influenced by negative influences we can create much trouble or we can be prevented from achieving our personal goals.

1502. It is necessary that every day, continuously, for as long as we live, to be influenced by positive constructive influences.

1503. Constructive influences help us greatly to the achievement of our personal goals.

1504. It is a shame not to leave ourselves influenced by positive influences if we have the chance.

1505. Positive influences influence us very much to achieve more and more successes.

1506. Positive influences influence us very much to expand opportunities so as to meet more favorable circumstances.

1507. To succeed in life it is necessary to guard yourself against negative influences.

1508. To succeed in life as well as we can it is necessary day by day, continuously, for as long as we live to have the personal goal to guard ourselves against negative influences.

1509. We have to take the necessary measures so that children can not be influenced by negative influences.

1510. If we are influenced by negative influences we have a lot to lose.

1511. If we are influenced by negative influences we make very big troubles or we are prevented from achieving our personal goals.

Ingenious

1512. The limits of achievement imposed by ourselves in our mind at a given moment can be overcome or eliminated also through the contribution of the formation, development, maintenance and usage of ingenious behavior.

1513. We can prevent the falling apart of a happy marriage also through the contribution of the formation, development, maintenance and usage of ingenious behavior.

1514. Rather than lamenting that we do not have successes it is more useful to also form, develop, maintain and use ingenious behavior.

1515. Our resistance to changing for the better can be overcome also through the contribution of the formation, development, maintenance and usage of ingenious behavior.

1516. In order to rise up once again for the first time for the who knows what time it is necessary to also form, develop, maintain and use ingenious behavior.

1517. In order to prevent not achieving our personal goals, it is necessary to also form, develop, maintain and use our ingenious behavior.

1518. We can form, develop and maintain the state of being ourselves also through the contribution of the formation, development, maintenance and usage of an ingenious behavior.

1519. Our future can be projected and achieved also through the contribution of the formation, development, maintenance and usage of ingenious behavior.

1520. In achieving our successes a contribution is also brought by the formation, development, maintenance and usage of ingenious behavior.

1521. We can prevent some failures also through the contribution of the formation, development, maintenance and usage of ingenious behavior.

1522. Hopes can be created also through the contribution of the formation, development, maintenance and usage of ingenious behavior.

1523. In order to escape poverty it is necessary to also form, develop, maintain and use ingenious behavior.

1524. Obtaining more and greater successes can be achieved also through the contribution of the formation, development, maintenance, usage of an ingenious behavior.

1525. The force of our ideas can be augmented also through the contribution of the formation, development, maintenance and usage of ingenious behavior.

1526. Some mistakes can be prevented also through the contribution of the formation, development, maintenance and usage of ingenious behavior.

1527. We can contribute to the achievement of our greatest accomplishments also through the contribution of the formation, development, maintenance and usage of ingenious behavior.

1528. Positive experience can be achieved also through the contribution of the formation, development, maintenance and usage of ingenious behavior.

Initiatives

1529. Countries should promote, encourage and finance more positive and effective initiatives of young people.

1530. The state's funding of more positive and effective initiatives, useful for the youth and for society would greatly reduce the number of young negative facts.

1531. The financing by the state of more positive, efficient initiatives, helpful to people and society should contribute a lot and would accelerate the development of their personality, their integration into society, from participating in the realization of many activities of society.

1532. Assuming initiatives helps us achieve more true friendships.

1533. Assuming initiatives helps us achieve more pleasant surprises.

1534. Assuming initiatives helps us achieve more personal goals.

1535. Assuming initiatives helps us achieve more records.

1536. Assuming initiatives helps us achieve more successes.

1537. Assuming initiatives helps us achieve more favorable chances.

1538. Assuming initiatives helps us achieve more favorable situations.

1539. Assuming initiatives helps us achieve much good luck.

Innovating

1540. People who have and innovating spirit have more potential to increase their efficiency.

1541. People who have an innovating spirit have more potential to find the right partner for life.

1542. People with an innovating spirit more easily achieve social relations.

1543. People with an innovating spirit more easily achieve efficient co operations.

1544. People with and innovating spirit have much more chances to meet more favorable situations.

1545. People with an innovating spirit have a great potential to participate in efficient global co operations.

Intellectual

1546. The more we develop our intellectual, the more likely we will not get to the situation of despair.

1547. We can have a positive thinking unless we do not have it, through a proper diet, education, intellectual exercises, perseverance, experience, desire, exercise, etc..

1548. Cheerfulness can not be achieved if you do not have a proper diet, education, intellectual exercise, perseverance, will, exercise, a system of values which we believe in and that we respect, business dynamism, social relations, friends, mature love, or a happy marriage.

1549. Weariness can be prevented through proper diet, education, positive behavior balanced intellectual exercise, perseverance, will, exercise, a value system that we believe in and that we respect, business dynamism, social relations, friends, mature love, a happy marriage, adequate rest when necessary, appropriate sleep, entertainment, etc.

1550. Intellectual qualities are also an effect of education.

1551. Intellectual qualities can be developed continuously, day by day, for as long as we live.

1552. Intellectual qualities are more important to succeed in life.

1553. Intellectual qualities help us the most to achieve many personal goals.

1554. The development of intellectual skills continuously, day by day, for as long as we live should be a personal goal for each of us.

1555. Intellectual qualities help us achieve effective co operations.

1556. An optimal morale can be formed through a proper diet, education, intellectual exercises, perseverance, will, physical exercises, etc.

1557. Good humor can be maintained through a balanced life, a proper diet, education, intellectual exercises, psychical balance, perseverance, women, physical exercises, a value system in which we believe in and that we respect, positive activities, dynamism, social relations, friends, mature love, a happy marriage, etc.

1558. Positive thinking can be maintained through a proper diet, education, intellectual exercise, perseverance, experience, will, physical exercises, etc.

1559. The more intellectually developed we are the more chances we have not to get to that state of despair.

1560. A psychological balance can be maintain once achieved through the proper nutrition of the person concerned, through education, intellectual work, perseverance, experience, willingness, physical exercises, etc.

1561. Positive thinking can be achieved if you do not have it through the proper nutrition of the person concerned, through education, intellectual work, perseverance, experience, willingness, physical exercises, etc.

Inventive

1562. We can prevent some failures also through the contribution of the formation, development, maintenance and usage of inventive behavior.

1563. We can prevent the falling apart of a happy marriage also through the contribution of the formation, development, maintenance and usage of inventive behavior.

1564. Obtaining more and greater successes can be achieved also through the contribution of the formation, development, maintenance, usage of an inventive behavior.

1565. The obstacles that prevent us from achieving our personal goals can be surpassed also through the contribution of the formation, development, maintenance and usage of inventive behavior.

1566. Acting efficiently helps us become inventive.

1567. Positive experience can be achieved also through the contribution of the formation, development, maintenance and usage of inventive behavior.

1568. Our own happiness can be achieved and maintained also through the contribution of the formation, development, maintenance and usage of inventive behavior.

1569. Problems cannot be solved by the ideas that created them but also through the contribution of the formation, development, maintenance and usage of inventive behavior.

1570. In achieving our successes a contribution is also brought by the formation, development, maintenance and usage of inventive behavior.

1571. We can form, develop and maintain the state of being ourselves also through the contribution of the formation, development, maintenance and usage of an inventive behavior.

1572. In order to escape poverty it is necessary to also form, develop, maintain and use inventive behavior.

1573. In order to prevent failures it is necessary to also form, develop, maintain and use inventive behavior.

1574. Release from our self-imposed restrictions can be made also through the contribution of the formation, development, maintenance and usage of inventive behavior.

1575. Hopes can be created also through the contribution of the formation, development, maintenance and usage of inventive behavior.

1576. Continuous self-motivation helps us become inventive.

1577. Our resistance to changing for the better can be overcome also through the contribution of the formation, development, maintenance and usage of inventive behavior.

1578. Pessimism can be removed and replaced with optimism also through the contribution of the formation, development, maintenance and usage of inventive behavior.

Invincible

1579. Through co operation we can become invincible much faster.

1580. All the people on this earth have sufficient resources through their huge resources, by unity, solidarity, co operation, co-development, perseverence, will, work, Internet, media, etc. to install itself in a record time in many places and situations, abnormalities instead of the normal. Get started now as you will always succeed because you are an invincible force, you can replace abnormalities with normal situations and places. Persevere until you succeed and if needed continually ask for the help of other citizens of the planet that you will be joined by incredibly many of them. Good luck. I am sure you will succeed.

1581. People on earth have sufficient resources to unite their huge forces, through solidarity, cooperation, co-development, perseverance, willpower, work, the Internet, the media, the mobile phone, etc., to install in record time in many places and situations normality instead of abnormalities. Start right now that you will always succeed for you are an invincible force, you can replace the abnormal with the normal in no matter what situations and places. Persevere until you succeed and if you need it, continually ask for help from other citizens of the planet that

will join you to become incredibly many.
Good luck. I am sure you will succeed.

Irresponsability

1582. The irresponsibility of many people stopped in a lot of ways until now, progress in many areas.

1583. All employees of international organizations and states, which act during the performance of their duties with irresponsibility should be dismissed immediately and effective measures to recover the damage created by their irresponsible actions should be taken.

1584. Leaders of countries have an enormous responsibility to the people, but unfortunately they often demonstrate very much and great irresponsibility.

1585. After a while, when they are divorced, they realize their irresponsibility, the enormous value that they had lost and that their children had lost.

1586. Unfortunately there are still enormously many people in functions with high responsibilities but who unfortunately prove much irresponsibility.

Keeping

1587. Cooperation is a factor of peacekeeping.

1588. The rigorous and disciplined at work have much greater opportunities to obtain and maintain employment. Rigor and discipline at the workplace can be easy if we want to, if we do not have it. Rigor and discipline are two keys to getting a job if you do not have it, or if we have one, they are keys to keeping it. Good luck.

1589. By doing what we should do we will succeed in keeping our marriage happy.

1590. Fatigue can be prevented by keeping in shape.

1591. Fairness increases our chances of keeping efficient co operations.

Knowledge

1592. Young people from many countries of the world by filling seats that they can in local councils, central ones, in the parliament, government and other institutions and by maximizing the use of the resources available (energy, enthusiasm, optimism, devotion, capacities, values, skills, abilities, knowledge, etc.) can contribute enormously much to accelerating the solving of many problems of their regims, of their goals, and of the world.

1593. The science of preventing human errors should include knowledge of prevention of human errors for each field of activity and every human action.

1594. Due to enormous progress of human knowledge that is continuously growing daily, daily, the number of new opportunities to create a better quality of life is getting better.

1595. Unfortunately, enormously many people are not concerned to find and use human knowledge that can help enormously hard to achieve a much better quality of life.

1596. Human knowledge should be used effectively, organized, planned, impersonal, humanist for the good of our people and, in an incredibly short time, the quality of life of billions of people would grow incredibly much.

1597. Most people today do not know how to use all of human knowledge that they could use to make their life much better.

1598. Each of us can come, by using the Internet, to get to know human knowledge that can help us greatly in increasing the quality of our life.

1599. While entering into relationships with other people it is good to take from them as much positive experience and knowledge as we can because they help us achieve the happiness that we all want for ourselves.

1600. The continuous search for positive and useful knowledge should be a primary objective of ours for as long as we live.

1601. Only positive and useful knowledge to us can help us continue to achieve positive realistic goals.

1602. Many people have a lot of failures in life because they do not have the necessary knowledge.

1603. The more knowledge we have of those needed to achieve personal objectives the more likely we are to achieve our objectives.

Life

1604. We can make life happier by respecting the rules that make our life happier.

1605. We can make life happier only when we respect the rules that make our life happier.

1606. Human experience accumulated so far, a part of it stored in books, on the Internet, etc.. gives and creates large opportunities for us to have a happy life if we study and depict it.

1607. Life should not be lived to make fun of it.

1608. It is never too late to start our family life all over again.

1609. It is never too late to start a new life all over again.

1610. Hypocrisy is a big flaw that harms us very much in life.

1611. Faith helps us very much in life.

1612. A grudge against another or others does not help us with anything in life.

1613. Helping others to become happy is one of the priority objectives of my life.

1614. Each of us has the chance to assert oneself in real life. It is important to discover the chances and to achieve the goal.

1615. The ideas of these books, magazines help us discover opportunities and the potential chances of life.

1616. True friendship can help us pass much easier over the many difficulties of life, and it would not be so if it did not exist.

1617. The desire to make one's way in life by any means is very harmful to anyone.

1618. One of the objectives of our life should be the harmonious development of our personality.

1619. In life it is fair and onest not to make promises that we know we cannot keep, because these facts damage both the one we make them to and ourselves as well.

1620. To succeed in life, we need preventive thinking.

1621. To have the least possible number of failures in our life it is also necessary to have a long-term thinking.

1622. To have the least possible failures in life is we need conversant as necessary to achieve personal goals, without having failures, in order to achieve them.

1623. To successfully face the needs of personal life, it is necessary to continuously learn while we live.

1624. Those who had a life filled with many successes, outstanding performance and records have learned with a maximum devotion during their life.

1625. Failures should never discourage us, because life also offers us many favorable situations to succeed. Through perseverance we will also find those favorable situations that will help us have success.

1626. Failures in life can be many times prevented also through a positive thought.

1627. Life would have much less trouble if we would be more careful in every action of ours.

Ardelean Gheorghe Cornel(BIGAGC)

Living

1628. By living our lives at random, happiness too can only be accomplished randomly.

1629. By good co-living, we can achieve much more successes.

1630. Society has no right to abandon its people who need protection without protection, without shelter, living on the streets, canals, etc.. without a minimum of shelter and food for a normal living.

1631. Many of the people living from hand to mouth are not happy.

1632. Most people living from hand to mouth are very easy to manipulate.

1633. Most people living from hand to mouth are not satisfied with the life that they lead.

1634. Most people living from hand to mouth do not feel that they are really alive.

1635. On the other hand there are many women who do the almost impossible to achieve and maintain happy marriages, to prevent divorce. These are, some of them, living models which deserve all the respect and appreciation in the world and they deserve to be known both them, by all of us, and their outstanding deeds in order to imitate them.

1636. The art of living can be learned through will, persistence, continuing education and effective actions to achieve the objectives.

1637. By living our lives at random we can also only achieve happiness at random.

1638. Each of us has had one or more bigger or smaller failures. It's good not to have any failures or as few failures as possible. Some or more failures could harm us very much. Those who were careful did not achieve failure or failures and have made smaller, fewer ones. Prevision helps us prevent many failures. The more experienced in previsioning we are, the greater ability we have to provide, as we have more knowledge necessary to achieve previsions etc.. the more we can make accurate previsions, prevent many mistakes, failures, trouble, accidents, conflicts, arguments, unsuccessful actions, etc. In our personal and professional life, it is necessary to continuously develop and to have that personal goal to develop to a maximum capacity the prevision in private life, the ability to use previsions. We can continuously increase the capacity of our prevision very much, as we live if we have personal objectives, as we expand our ability to prevision and whether we act to continuously and effectively achieve this objective. Those who aimed at personal living as to develop the capacity of prevision continuously and concretely act with dedication to achieve their capacity to make a prevision which will help them achieve one or more very big successes, they will succeed to prevent many failures, troubles, etc., they will be able to achieve much in life, to have many happy, satisfying moments and so much happiness. The more we have a capacity of more than prevision, a more accurate, more efficient one, the more valuable we are for having this treasure. This treasure we can continuously increase greatly. The capacity of prevision generally contains more capacities of prevision in some actions, behaviors in the achievement of personal objectives, private, professional, specific ones, etc. It is necessary to develop those capabilities specific to prediction that we need. Knowledge, experience, qualifications, skills, etc., in a specific prevision capacity can be used to a greater or lesser degree in other capacities specific to prevision. The capacities of prevision are very necessary and very useful to us but unfortunately very few people have personal goals in life to continuously develop the specific performance of prevision. Due to the special importance of the capacity of prevision it is necessary and required to create and develop the science of the development of the capacity of prevision, because having this science we would have it by applying enormous positive effects on countless people that should develop and apply it indirectly on other people. The state would accelerate progress in many fields, would accelerate the reduction of illiteracy, poverty, illness, divorces out of arguments and conflict, accidents, what harms humans, animals, the environment, etc.. It would lead to solving many personal and state targets, it would create enormously many joys, much satisfaction and happiness. It would lead to the situation that most people no longer live at the whim of chance, with no personal, professional security, etc.. but on the contrary they would lead to more people having them as an objective and as they continue to live, they would develop the personal capacities necessary for their prevision and apply them every day, both in the establishment of private personal or professional life, it would be something concrete that will help them achieve more harmonious lives to achieve what they want and need for their families.

1639. There is the capacity of prevision in specific persons, specific societies, specific legal entities, nonprofit organizations, companies, banks, groups, collectivities, international and intergovernmental organizations. Both individuals and legal entities, must not live from hand to mouth, must act firmly, must study and evaluate the effects of positive and negative actions, decisions, etc. their objectives are also necessary to be: 1) to aim at continuing to develop their capacities of specific prediction that they need. 2) to apply, continuous use in any action, situation-specific prediction capabilities necessary and useful efforts, energy consumption and costs for the development and capacity of specific prevision that they need.

1640. Failures can happen in each of our actions or less often. Our failures can be created by factors and actions sometimes difficult to identify and prevent. However there are actions where we can know all the factors that can create failures. Knowing the factors that create failures in actions, we can take the necessary measures to prevent them by reaching in some cases to zero failures, as they have succeeded in situations in a long time, in many states, especially people in the most developed countries of the world. How to develop more this science with the more than we can know more of the factors that could cause failures in certain situations to certain actions. Scientific knowledge can contribute greatly to preventing many failures in many actions. At present people do not use scientific knowledge, the human experience gained in books, studies, on the Internet, although they have committed enormously many failures, mistakes, although they could prevent many huge mistakes, failures if they would use efficient, organized, timely human experience and knowledge from books, the Internet when they would need it. Countries should take immediate measures and be more interested in people and use them when they need knowledge and human experience that can reach and can be used. Human knowledge is growing and increases daily awfully much, and human experience which can create the situation so that we can prevent every day more even more mistakes and failures with positive effects on our high society, to accelerate progress in many areas.

1641. Where we have failures we should never discourage and lose our wits, our balance inside, our optimism, morale or to start to grieve. If we do this, it would solve absolutely no problem, but on the contrary, it would stress us illogically, abnormally without any positive effects. Those who have achieved many successes knew how to cope with failure, learning from failures, to reduce the negative effects of failures. Many failures rather than strengthening us, they weaken us, they should give us power instead of imobilizing us and mobilize us instead of making them harder to give motivation, instead of multiple negative effects they should have have multiple positive effects.

1642. However, I disagree and do not consider as logical, positive or constructive the popular saying: „Man learns from mistakes". Man, on the contrary should learn only from his successes and from those who have achieved successes and gained, by imitating those positive behaviors, which have effectively contributed to success. In addition man can learn enormously not to have failures, or make mistakes from the knowledge and positive experience of mankind stored in books, media, on the Internet and the experience of people who have huge experience and knowledge. The more we can prevent more failures, mistakes, the more we can prevent more and more different negative effects.

1643. It would be necessary and useful the development of a science to prevent human errors because it would prevent a large number of human errors and failures if people study and apply it as much and in as many actions as they can. This knowledge could and should be studied in colleges and universities and other educational forms. In every area of activity for each action type, it could identify factors that create human mistakes and failures and then it could identify solutions and measures to be taken to prevent mistakes and failures.

1644. Efforts and expenses that will be done by creating, developing, learning and applicating the science to prevent human errors will not be much lower than the positive effects of their prevention of a very large number of mistakes and failures and their multiple, diverse and very large negative effects. Financial investment, energy, time, etc.. in these activities related to the prevention of human errors and failures would be very effective and necessary and useful for both countries and for people in particular. Each of us in a greater or lesser way can participate in the creation, development and application of the science to prevent human errors.

1645. Those who are independent earn their own living.

1646. Some people only pretend to be living, but they practically mock themselves and their life.

1647. It is much more pleasant to have sex with your partner than living in a temporary extra-conjugal relationship.

1648. Each parent is required to ensure continuously, day by day, living conditions for the necessary growth and education of his children and for the harmonious development of their personality.

1649. Happiness makes us eager to keep living.

1650. Self- control is a quality very necessary and very appreciated for shared living.

1651. The future possibilities of living are unlimited for most of the population.

1652. A man with practical values succeeds in earning his living for life.

1653. A man with self control earns his living.

1654. People with tact know how to earn their living.

1655. Positive living models impel us a lot to proceed to action.

1656. Each of us needs to know to distinguish between what is necessary to do in order to earn our living and to succeed in life.

1657. People who have had success have given up living in the state of fatigue.

1658. Humanist scientific knowledge, human living experience, stored in books, on the Internet, in the media, human qualities allow the achievement of an incredibly high number of happy marriages, but, unfortunately, many people do not give the time and the attention necessary to achieving and maintaining a happy marriage.

1659. A man who acts continuously, day by day to become even more economic will certainly succeed to earn his living in life.

1660. An honest man manages to earn his living in life.

1661. Industrious people certainly earn their living in life on their own.

1662. People who have been in prison rightfully or wrongfully, and after being released they have succeeded, they must become living models for every person no matter what their status is, either head of state or a person in prison.

Logically

1663. A great capacity of analyzing a situation logically helps us maintain our way of being loved.

1664. A great capacity of analyzing a situation logically helps us become more humane.

1665. A great capacity of analyzing a situation logically helps us maintain our wisdom.

1666. We can form, develop and maintain the state of being ourselves also through the contribution of the formation, development, maintenance and usage of a logical behavior.

1667. Continuous self-motivation helps us become logical.

1668. In order to prevent not achieving our personal goals, it is necessary to also form, develop, maintain and use our logical behavior.

1669. A great capacity of analyzing a situation logically helps us become more pleasant.

1670. A great capacity of analyzing a situation logically helps us become more cautious.

1671. A great capacity of analyzing a situation logically helps us become more loved.

1672. A great capacity of analyzing a situation logically helps us become more preventive.

1673. A great capacity of analyzing a situation logically helps us maintain our way of being understanding.

1674. Acting efficiently helps us become logical.

1675. Positive experience can be achieved also through the contribution of the formation, development, maintenance and usage of logic behavior.

1676. A great capacity of analyzing a situation logically helps us maintain our happiness.

1677. Some mistakes can be prevented also through the contribution of the formation, development, maintenance and usage of logic behavior.

1678. A great capacity of analyzing a situation logically helps us become productive.

1679. A great capacity of analyzing a situation logically must be developed.

1680. A great capacity of analyzing a situation logically helps us become more tolerant.

1681. Our future can be projected and achieved also through the contribution of the formation, development, maintenance and usage of logical behavior.

1682. In achieving our successes a contribution is also brought by the formation, development, maintenance and usage of logical behavior.

1683. We can overcome the difficulties that we must overcome also through the help of the formation, development, maintenance and usage of logical behavior.

1684. A great capacity of analyzing a situation logically helps us become more understanding.

1685. A great capacity of analyzing a situation logically helps us maintain our way of being practical.

1686. Problems cannot be solved by the ideas that created them but also through the contribution of the formation, development, maintenance and usage of logical behavior.

1687. We can contribute to the achievement of our greatest accomplishments also through the contribution of the formation, development, maintenance and usage of logical behavior.

1688. A great capacity of analyzing a situation logically helps us achieve more successes.

1689. Obtaining more and greater successes can be achieved also through the contribution of the formation, development, maintenance, usage of a logical behavior.

1690. We can become stronger and we can not allow ourselves to be influenced by the world also through the contribution of the formation, development, maintenance and usage of logical behavior.

1691. Rather than lamenting that we do not have successes it is more useful to also form, develop, maintain and use logical behavior.

1692. A great capacity of analyzing a situation logically must be maintained.

1693. A great capacity of analyzing a situation logically helps us become understanding.

1694. In order to prevent failures it is necessary to also form, develop, maintain and use logical behavior.

1695. A great capacity of analyzing a situation logically helps us maintain our way of being liked.

1696. Our happiness depends a lot also on the formation, development, maintenance and usage of logical behavior.

1697. A great capacity of analyzing a situation logically helps us maintain our way of being loving.

1698. A great capacity of analyzing a situation logically helps us become happy.

1699. A great capacity of analyzing a situation logically helps us maintain our optimism.

Long-term

1700. The effects of human actions have an increasing influence on the environment. This makes us think on a global scale, long-term and scientific before acting and makes us perform more profound studies, of impact, regarding our actions, to prevent the implementation of actions that have negative, inadmissible effects on the environment, society and people.

1701. To have the least possible number of failures in our life it is also necessary to have a long-term thinking.

1702. We can prevent many failures can with the help of long-term thinking.

1703. Thinking long-term helps us to prevent many mistakes.

1704. We can prevent a very large number of inefficient actions with a long-term thinking.

1705. Incredible facts are made mostly by people who have long-term objectives and work with dedication to achieve them.

1706. Short-term thinking is necessary to be combined with long-term thinking.

1707. The great and special achievements of mankind have been carried out by people who have used long-term thinking.

1708. It is necessary and required that society develops studies and research about the future, thinking futurologically, long-term projects for faster implementation and development of some theories, a more complete knowledge of them to be able to handle projects for the future and prevent mistakes made previously by society.

1709. Long-term thinking is specific to futurological thinking.

1710. Hopes make us form our long-term thinking.

1711. Thinking long-term helps and contributes greatly to increasing our confidence in us.

1712. A man with a broad horizon most of the times has a long-term thinking.

1713. People with human social behaviors have a long-term thinking.

1714. People with no hopes for the future need to connect with those who have a long-term thinking.

1715. In order to escape poverty it is necessary to form, develop, maintain and use long-term thinking.

1716. Hopes can be created by using a long-term thinking.

Maintain

1717. The necessary abilities, including those necessary to achieve our personal goals, can be formed, developed, maintained and used also through the contribution of the formation, development, maintenance and usage have the ability to organize efficiently.

1718. In order to take correct decisions it is necessary that we form, develop, maintain and use the ability to be responsible.

1719. Courage can be created, developed, increased, maintained and used also through the contribution of the formation, development, maintenance and usage of an objective behavior.

1720. Will can be formed, developed, maintained and used also through the contribution of the formation, development, maintenance and usage of the capacity of self-control.

1721. Discipline can be formed, developed, maintained and used also through the contribution of the formation, development, maintenance and usage of the ability to organize.

1722. Our qualities can be formed, developed, maintained and used also through the contribution of the formation, development, maintenance and usage of global thinking.

1723. Those who do not think enough need to form, develop, maintain and use constructive thinking.

1724. Abilities can be formed, developed, maintained and used also through the contribution of the formation, development, maintenance and usage of cooperative behaviors.

1725. By listening very carefully to what people who have had successes say and by taking useful ideas from them we can form, develop, maintain and use a positive conception of life.

1726. In order to prevent not achieving our personal goals it is necessary to form, develop, maintain and use only optimistic ideas.

1727. Abilities can be formed, developed, maintained and used also through the contribution of the formation, development, maintenance and usage of the ability of rapid perception.

1728. We can form, develop, maintain and use an open mind also through the contribution of the formation, development, maintenance and usage of anticipative behavior.

1729. By listening very carefully to what people who have had successes say and by taking useful ideas from them we can form, develop, maintain and use the ideas of that help us motivate ourselves.

1730. Rather than lamenting that we do not have successes it is better to form, develop and maintain a realistic thinking.

1731. Forming wrong ideas can be prevented also through the formation, development, maintenance and usage of the ability to maintain efficient collaborations.

1732. In order to pursue and transform our personal goals into reality we need to form, develop, maintain and use anticipative thinking.

1733. A reliable man has great chances of maintaining his marriage happy.

1734. The ability to react with understanding helps us a lot to maintain a happy marriage.

1735. A quiet and reserved man has great chances of maintaining a happy marriage.

1736. People who are forgiving know how to maintain a true mature love.

1737. Efficient communication contributes a lot to maintaining social relations.

1738. Those who value their collaborators have a greater potential to maintain their marriage happy.

1739. The ability to adopt visions helps us maintain an efficient co-development.

1740. The ability of optimal adaptation increases our possibilities maintain a happy marriage.

1741. A man ready at any time to help someone has more chances to maintain a happy marriage.

1742. The desire to succeed in life helps us a lot to maintain a happy marriage.

1743. A balanced marriage is also maintained with the help of positive exchanges of information.

1744. Without an efficient human communication efficient co operations cannot be maintained.

1745. The sense of organization contributes a lot to maintaining efficient collaboration.

1746. The sense of organization contributes a lot to maintaining efficient co operations.

1747. Those who build a life on the basis of rational consciousness have greater chances to maintain a happy marriage.

1748. Those who value their collaborators have a greater potential to maintain a happy marriage.

1749. Those who value their collaborators have a greater potential to maintain true friendships.

1750. Developing the ability of listening increases our chances of maintaining a happy marriage.

1751. The sense of responsibility contributes a lot to maintaining a mature true love.

1752. An efficient communication contributes a lot to maintaining a happy marriage.

1753. People who are used to carrying out the activities they have started more easily and surely maintain a mature love.

1754. A good state of health contributes a lot to maintaining efficiency.

1755. Those who have the sense of objectivity are also capable of maintaining a mature love.

1756. People with prejudices, because of some prejudices have no way of maintaining some efficient co-developments.

1757. A low tolerance for personal imperfections helps us a lot to maintain a happy marriage.

1758. Those who truly love people have much more chances to maintain a happy marriage.

1759. An understanding man has more chances to maintain a happy marriage.

1760. A man's need for safety makes many people maintain true friendships.

1761. The sense of responsibility contributes a lot in maintaining a happy marriage.

1762. People who are used to carry out the activities they have started more easily maintain true friendships.

1763. Those who truly love people have much more chances to maintain efficient co-developments.

1764. A peaceful man through his behavior contributes a lot to maintaining a happy marriage.

1765. Continuous self-perfection increases our possibilities to maintain a happy marriage.

1766. Our necessary capacities including those necessary to the achievement of personal objectives can be formed, developed, maintained and used through the contribution of the formation, development, maintenance and usage of the ability to efficiently organize.

1767. It is best to form, develop, maintain and use our realistic thinking.

Meditations

1768. My meditations give us an impulse to achieve our personal goals. Read, analyze them and apply those you accept. Good luck.

1769. My meditations push us, give us impulses to do only what is good for us, for others, and for society. Read, analyze them and apply those you accept. Good luck.

1770. My meditations push us, give us impulses to achieve a better life. Read, analyze them and apply those you accept. Good luck.

1771. My meditations push us, give us impulses to take care of us, of our health, of our family etc. Read, analyze them and apply those you accept. Good luck.

1772. My meditations push us, give us impulses to do what is necessary and required. Read, analyze them and apply those you accept. Good luck.

1773. My meditations push us, give us impulses to achieve a better world. Read, analyze them and apply those you accept. Good luck.

1774. My meditations help us achieve and maintain a happy marriage. Read, analyze and apply those that you accept. Good luck.

1775. My meditations help us achieve and maintain true love. Read, analyze and apply those that you accept. Good luck.

1776. My meditations impulse us, push us to achieve and maintain a happy marriage.

Read, analyze and apply those that you accept. Good luck.

1777. My meditations impulse us and push us to achieve and maintain true love. Read, analyze and apply those that you accept. Good luck.

1778. My meditations impulse us, push us to succeed in life. Read, analyze and apply those that you accept. Good luck.

1779. Meditations develop our common sense.

1780. Meditations make us give more attention and time in all that concerns us.

1781. Meditations help us make a more beautiful life.

1782. Meditations help us achieve happy marriages.

1783. By reading and applying some meditations written by me, these help us educate and raise our children better.

1784. By reading and applying some meditations written by me, we take more care of our children, of those that we love and of others.

Mentalities

1785. The negative mentalities of those who have them make it very difficult to achieve personal goals.

1786. The negative mentalities of those who have them make it very difficult to achieve efective co operations.

1787. If you unfortunately have some negative mentalities (which may be crimes) is good to stop their use.

1788. Negative mentalities make those who prevent them deserving to have some successes.

1789. Some behaviors, called mentalities, are not in fact mentalities, but crimes.

1790. If you unfortunately have some negative mentalities (which may be crimes) it is better to stop using them.

1791. Negative mentalities for those who do not prevent them keep them from having some successes that they could achieve.

1792. Negative mentalities make it very hard for us to achieve successes.

1793. Negative mentalities make it very hard to do effective actions.

1794. Those with negative mentalities do not achieve effective co-developments.

1795. Negative mentalities of those who have them greatly slow the achievement of personal goals.

1796. Negative mentalities of those who have them slow the achievement of effective co operations.

Methods

1797. Those who solve problems only through constructive methods contribute a lot in achieving the greater good.

1798. Those who solve problems only through constructive methods have more chances to meet more favorable situations.

1799. Those who solve problems only through constructive methods have more chances to achieve happy marriages.

1800. Solving problems through positive methods contributes a lot in achieving the greater good.

1801. Solving problems through positive methods is also done with the help of exchanging information.

1802. Solving problems through positive methods must be promoted.

1803. Solving problems through positive methods helps us a lot in achieving our personal goals.

1804. Solving problems through positive methods increases our capacity to maintain a mature love.

1805. Solving problems through positive methods increases our abilities to achieve efficient co-developments.

1806. Those who only solve problems through constructive methods have a greater ability to achieve their own happiness.

1807. Those who only solve problems through constructive methods must be appreciated.

1808. Those who only solve problems through constructive methods prevent many failures.

1809. Solving problems only through constructive methods increases our credibility.

1810. Preventing problems through positive methods increases our chances to participate in achieving efficient global co operations.

1811. Solving problems through positive methods must be appreciated.

1812. Solving problems through positive methods helps us a lot to contribute to global humanization.

1813. Those who solve their problems only through constructive methods have greater chances to succeed in life.

1814. Those who solve their problems only through constructive methods must be promoted.

1815. Those who solve their problems only through constructive methods have greater chances to achieve efficient co-developments.

1816. Those who solve their problems only through constructive methods have chances to achieve outstanding performances.

1817. Those who only solve problems through constructive methods have a greater ability to maintain those constructive methods.

1818. Those who solve problems only through constructive methods make many exchanges of information.

1819. Those who solve problems only through constructive methods have more chances to find the right partner for life.

1820. Solving problems through positive methods does not create problems with the law.

1821. Solving problems through positive methods does not create other problems in an illegal way.

1822. Solving problems through positive methods is an obligation of every individual.

1823. Solving problems through positive methods does not make building our desired future much more difficult.

1824. Solving problems through positive methods is a necessity for each of us.

Meticulous

1825. We can form, develop and maintain the state of being ourselves also through the contribution of the formation, development, maintenance and usage of a meticulous behavior.

1826. Our resistance to changing for the better can be overcome also through the contribution of the formation, development, maintenance and usage of meticulous behavior.

1827. In order to prevent not achieving our personal goals, it is necessary to also form, develop, maintain and use our meticulous behavior.

1828. Our own happiness can be achieved and maintained also through the contribution of the formation, development, maintenance and usage of meticulous behavior.

1829. Our future can be projected and achieved also through the contribution of the formation, development, maintenance and usage of meticulous behavior.

1830. The radical transformation for the better of our life can be achieved also through the formation, development, maintenance and usage of meticulous behavior.

1831. The force of our ideas can be augmented also through the contribution of the formation, development, maintenance and usage of meticulous behavior.

1832. We can contribute to the achievement of our greatest accomplishments also through the contribution of the formation, development, maintenance and usage of meticulous behavior.

1833. In order to escape poverty it is necessary to also form, develop, maintain and use meticulous behavior.

1834. Some mistakes can be prevented also through the contribution of the formation, development, maintenance and usage of meticulous behavior.

1835. Aspiring towards a more meaningful life can also be achieved through the formation, development, maintenance and usage of meticulous behavior.

1836. Responsibility helps us become meticulous.

1837. Continuous self-motivation helps us become meticulous.

1838. The self efficient use of our time helps us become meticulous.

1839. We can overcome the difficulties that we must overcome also through the help of the formation, development, maintenance and usage of meticulous behavior.

1840. Acting efficiently helps us become meticulous.

1841. Continuously making ourselves efficient helps us become meticulous.

1842. In achieving our successes a contribution is also brought by the formation, development, maintenance and usage of meticulous behavior.

1843. Confidence in ourselves helps us become meticulous.

1844. Hope helps us become meticulous.

1845. Our happiness depends a lot also on the formation, development, maintenance and usage of meticulous behavior.

1846. Will helps us become meticulous.

1847. Pessimism can be removed and replaced with optimism also through the contribution of the formation, development, maintenance and usage of meticulous behavior.

1848. The necessary qualities in achieving personal goals can be formed, developed, maintained and used also through the contribution of the formation, development, maintenance and usage of meticulous behavior.

1849. Hopes can be created also through the contribution of the formation, development, maintenance and usage of meticulous behavior.

1850. Rather than lamenting that we do not have successes it is more useful to also form, develop, maintain and use meticulous behavior.

1851. In order to prevent failures it is necessary to also form, develop, maintain and use meticulous behavior.

1852. Continuous self-control helps us become meticulous.

Misfortunes

1853. Anger has created many misfortunes.

1854. When we think constructively not destructively, we think this helps us prevent many mistakes, failures, accidents, divorces, misfortunes, conflicts, which are bad, harmful to us or others.

1855. Routine is very necessary and useful in behavior, etc. in actions for a certain period of time. After a certain period of time, at a certain time it is necessary to get rid of a certain routine, a certain behavior, a way of thinking, a certain kind of action, etc.. and replace it with another behavior more efficiently, more operational, more tactful, more thoughtful, etc.. in order to progress in achieving what we proposed, our personal objectives. When we need to get rid, to escape a certain routine it is necessary to get rid of it immediately, without doubts, delay, fears, etc. and to act in the new action, new behavior more effectively, without any delay. People who have the ability to leave a certain routine immediately when they need to, progress much faster in life, carry out much faster and more efficient personal goals, performe in live many more bigger or smaller successes than those who do not get rid of a particular or specific routine when necessary. Routine, when we get rid of it when necessary is a big negative factor of progress, it creates many failures, misfortunes, difficulties in achieving personal goals in life, it creates misunderstandings in families and may even lead to divorce, misunderstandings and even conflicts between large generations etc.. The routine of a normal fact, when we can not get rid of it, and it is necessary to get rid of it, it may actually become a very harmful fact for our new family, for the people around, for society, for younger generations and for the future, it may sometimes have many negative effects, very large and very diverse ones. For these reasons it is necessary to continuously develop our ability to get rid of routine when needed immediately.

1856. Weariness can produce very big misfortunes if we act when we are tired.

1857. Ignorance is a factor of many misfortunes.

1858. Negative thinking is the creative of many human misfortunes.

1859. Self- control prevents many misfortunes.

1860. Immorality is a question of many misfortunes.

1861. Thoughtless actions of people have unfortunately created a huge number of misfortunes and disasters.

1862. Unfortunately, a number of lawyers should be behind bars because of the many crimes they have done, because of the misfortunes and damage they have done, because of illegal behaviors in their relationship with their clients.

1863. Illegal actions of justice create many damages, misfortunes, sufferings and injustices.

1864. Humanist ideas prevent many misfortunes.

1865. Sometimes some ideas prevent many misfortunes.

1866. Lack of common sense leads to more misfortunes.

1867. Meanness is the cause of many misfortunes.

Mistakes

1868. People who have the ability to prevent possible mistakes achieve efficient co operations.

1869. People who have the ability to prevent possible mistakes obtain happy marriages.

1870. People who have the ability to prevent possible mistakes achieve efficient co-developments.

1871. People who have the ability to prevent possible mistakes find their right partner for life.

1872. People who have the ability to prevent possible mistakes can achieve a happy life.

1873. Those who live life passionately and not at random make fewer mistakes.

1874. Most of those who wander without a purpose in life make more mistakes.

1875. Correct thinking helps us a lot to prevent many possible mistakes.

1876. In order to change the desire of changing into reality it is necessary to form, develop, maintain and use the ability to prevent mistakes.

1877. We can prevent some mistakes also through the formation, development, maintenance and usage of the ability to select positive ideas.

1878. Some mistakes can be prevented also through the contribution of the formation, development, maintenance and usage of only positive ideas.

1879. Some mistakes can be prevented also through the contribution of the formation, development, maintenance and usage of a positive conception of life.

1880. We can prevent some mistakes also through the formation of the formation, development, maintenance and usage of the ability to develop our skills.

1881. We can prevent some mistakes also through the formation of the formation, development, maintenance and usage of the ability to motivate ourselves.

1882. Some mistakes can be sometimes prevented also through the contribution of the formation, development, maintenance and usage of efficient behaviors.

1883. Some mistakes can be prevented sometimes also through the formation, development, maintenance and usage of nondiscriminatory behavior.

1884. We can prevent some mistakes also through the formation of the formation, development, maintenance and usage of the ability of solving problems on time.

1885. We can prevent some mistakes also through the formation of the formation, development, maintenance and usage of the sense of quality in everything we do.

1886. We can prevent some mistakes also through the formation of the formation, development, maintenance and usage of anticipative thinking.

1887. We can prevent some mistakes also through the formation of the formation, development, maintenance and usage of the sense of commitment in everything we do.

1888. Some mistakes can be prevented sometimes also through the contribution of the formation, development, maintenance and usage of corresponding behaviors that are imposed by the situation.

1889. Some mistakes can be sometimes prevented also through the contribution of the formation, development, maintenance and usage of a predictable behavior.

1890. In order to pursue and transform our personal goals into reality we need to form, develop, maintain and use the ability to prevent mistakes.

1891. In order to escape poverty it is necessary to form, develop, maintain and use the ability to prevent mistakes.

1892. We can prevent some mistakes also through the contribution of the formation, development, maintenance and usage of constructive ideas.

1893. We can prevent some mistakes also through the formation of the formation, development, maintenance and usage of attentive behavior.

1894. Positive experience can be achieved also through the contribution of the formation, development and maintenance of the ability to prevent mistakes.

1895. We can prevent some mistakes also through the contribution of the formation, development, maintenance and usage of mature behaviors.

1896. Some mistakes can be prevented some times also through the contribution of the formation, development, maintenance and usage of behaviors imposed by the situation.

1897. In order to pursue and transform our personal goals into reality we need to form and develop the ability to prevent possible mistakes.

1898. We can prevent mistakes through responsible behaviors.

1899. Some mistakes can be prevented by finding their causes.

1900. Some mistakes can be prevented also through the contribution of formation, development, maintenance and usage of only positive ideas.

1901. We can prevent some mistakes also through the contribution of the formation, development, maintenance and usage of a positive life conception.

1902. Some mistakes can be prevented by using positive ideas.

1903. We can prevent some mistakes by adopting legal behaviors.

Mobilize

1904. The ability to mobilize is a creative attitude that helps us become more creative.

1905. Failures must never immobilize us.

1906. A man who has the ability to mobilize people most of the times achieves his financial independence.

1907. A man who has the ability to mobilize people contributes very much to the harmonious development of the people he coordinates.

1908. A man who has the ability to mobilize people has great chances to achieve lasting successes.

1909. An uncertainty of income immobilizes people.

1910. The desire of recognition and training mobilizes people to achieve successes.

1911. A man who has the ability to mobilize people has great chances of having a life full of successes.

1912. A sociable man many times has the power to mobilize people in a positive way.

1913. A man who has the ability to mobilize people influences progress in many areas of activity.

1914. A man who has the ability to mobilize people has more chances to change life for the better for many people.

1915. A man who has the ability to mobilize people must know how to efficiently manage his time.

1916. A man who has the ability to mobilize people contributes to achieving many of those people's dreams.

1917. In order to trace and transform our personal goals into reality it is necessary to form, develop, maintain and use the ability to mobilize people.

1918. Abilities can be formed, developed, maintained and used also through the contribution of the formation, development, maintenance and usage of the ability to mobilize.

1919. In order to pursue and transform our personal goals into reality we need to form, develop, maintain and use the ability to mobilize people.

1920. In order to prevent failures we must form, develop, maintain and use the ability to mobilize people.

Prevision

1921. Efforts and expenses that will be done by creating, developing, learning and applicating the science to prevent human errors will not be much lower than the positive effects of their prevention of a very large number of mistakes and failures and their multiple, diverse and very large negative effects. Financial investment, energy, time, etc.. in these activities related to the prevention of human errors and failures would be very effective and necessary and useful for both countries and for people in particular. Each of us in a greater or lesser way can participate in the creation, development and application of the science to prevent human errors.

1922. Abilities can be formed through prevision.

1923. In order to follow and transform our personal goals into reality, it is necessary to also form, develop, maintain and use our prevision.

Preventive

1924. Using preventive thinking increases our chances to succeed.

1925. Using preventive thinking increases our participation in achieving the greater good.

1026. Using preventive thinking helps us a lot in life.

1927. Preventive thinking must be promoted.

1928. Using preventive thinking helps us achieve our own happiness.

1929. Using preventive thinking contributes to the development of global thinking.

1930. Using preventive thinking helps in the achievement of some positive social relations.

1931. Preventive thinking contributes a lot in achieving efficient co operations.

1932. Using preventive thinking requires many exchanges of information.

1933. Preventive thinking must be maintained.

1934. People who have had successes mostly have a preventive thinking.

1935. Positive thinking helps us a lot to continuously be preventive.

1936. Preventive thinking is a necessity.

1937. Preventive thinking has a great contribution in achieving the desired future.

1938. Using preventive thinking is an obligation.

1939. The use of preventive thinking is an engine of development in all areas of activity.

1940. Using preventive thinking makes us more credible.

1941. Using preventive thinking makes us commit fewer mistakes.

1942. Preventive thinking must be rewarded.

1943. Humanist economy will greatly develop preventive economy.

1944. A man who knows how to protect himself permanently takes preventive measures.

1945. Forming wrong ideas about what is happening to us can be prevented also through the contribution of the formation, development, maintenance and usage of preventive thinking.

1946. We can overcome the difficulties that we need to overcome also through the formation, development and maintenance of preventive thinking.

1947. Those who are remarkably gifted many times have a preventive thinking.

Success

1948. Confidence in the success of what we do helps us achieve more favorable chances.

1949. A great capacity of assuming the necessary risks for success helps us maintain our happiness.

1950. A great capacity of assuming the necessary risks for success helps us maintain our way of being loving.

Selfishness

1951. Selfishness harms us a lot.

1952. Selfishness is one of the behaviors that stop the achievement of efficient co operations.

1953. Selfishness is one of the behaviors that stop the solving of many human problems.

Spontaneous

1954. People who have success voluntarily assume only when they have spontaneous successes the achievement of the goal.

1955. In order to follow and transform our personal goals into reality, it is necessary to also form, develop, maintain and use our spontaneous behavior.

1956. Hope helps us become spontaneous.

1957. The force of our ideas can be augmented also through the contribution of the formation, development, maintenance and usage of spontaneous behavior.

1958. Stress can be prevented also through the formation, development, maintenance and usage of spontaneous behavior.

1959. We can form, develop and maintain the state of being ourselves also through the contribution of the formation, development, maintenance and usage of a spontaneous behavior.

1960. In order to escape poverty it is necessary to also form, develop, maintain and use spontaneous behavior.

1961. Communication helps us become spontaneous.

1962. Creativity helps us become spontaneous.

1963. Will helps us become spontaneous.

1964. Obtaining more and greater successes can be achieved also through the contribution of the formation, development, maintenance, usage of a spontaneous behavior.

1965. The solutions to the problems we have or that we want to solve can be found also through the contribution of the formation, development, maintenance and usage of spontaneous behavior.

1966. Cherishing oneself helps us become spontaneous.

1967. Aspiring towards a more meaningful life can also be achieved through the formation, development, maintenance and usage of spontaneous behavior.

1968. Positive experience can be achieved also through the contribution of the formation, development, maintenance and usage of spontaneous behavior.

1969. Optimism helps us become spontaneous.

1970. Self-imposed discipline helps us become spontaneous.

1971. Our own happiness can be achieved and maintained also through the contribution of the formation, development, maintenance and usage of spontaneous behavior.

1972. In order to prevent not achieving our personal goals, it is necessary to also form, develop, maintain and use our spontaneous behavior.

Sorrows

1973. Mental self-development is of enormous help in preventing a lot of failures, sorrows, mistakes, illnesses, accidents, conflicts, arguments, divorces, negative actions, inefficiencies, etc.

1974. Our objectivity helps us prevent many sorrows.

1975. We can prevent sorrows through a positive thinking.

1976. Frequent sorrows are bad for our health.

1977. Sorrows sometimes complicate problems even more.

1978. Sorrows that are often do us much harm.

Stress

1979. Stress can be prevented also through the formation, development, maintenance and usage of diplomatic behavior.

1980. Stress can be prevented also through the formation, development, maintenance and usage of sturdy behavior.

1981. Stress can be prevented also through the formation, development, maintenance and usage of efficient behavior.

1982. Stress can be prevented also through the formation, development, maintenance and usage of persevering behavior.

1983. People who are resistant to stress have more chances to contribute to increasing the efficiency of the group they are in.

1984. Sociable individuals are more resistant to stress than lonely people.

1985. Those who are not stressed are less wrong.

1986. Those who are not stressed have fewer failures.

1987. Laugh prevents stress.

1988. Laugh helps us reduce stress.

1989. Good humor prevents stress.

1990. Cheerfulness prevents stress.

1991. Continuous, long, sometimes much stress leads some people into depression.

1992. Cheerfulness helps us get rid of stress.

Vision

1993. Each of us must make a vision of our own future.

1994. Unfortunately, some televisions promote very harmful negatives models of behavior.

1995. The ability of adopting visions is a quality that helps us establish our personal objectives.

1996. The ability of adopting visions is a quality that helps us achieve more easily more and greater successes.

1997. The ability of adopting visions helps us a lot in achieving efficient co operations.

1998. A strategic vision increases our chances of achieving personal goals.

1999. A strategic vision increases our trust in ourselves.

2000. A strategic vision makes us more effective.

2001. The ability of adopting visions helps us a lot to maintain efficient co operations.

2002. A strategic vision increases our chances to achieve a more beautiful future.

2003. A strategic vision increases our chances to achieve a more safe future.

2004. A strategic vision increases our chances of achieving efficient co-developments.

2005. The strategic vision helps us prevent many traps.

2006. A strategic vision helps us maintain a happy marriage.

2007. The ability to adopt visions helps us a lot to achieve our personal goals.

2008. The ability to adopt visions helps us a lot to have more chances to meet more favorable situations.

2009. The ability to adopt visions helps us a lot in achieving efficient co-developments.

2010. The ability to adopt visions helps us maintain an efficient co-development.

Ardelean Gheorghe Cornel(BIGAGC)

Biography

Ardelean Gheorghe Cornel(BIGAGC)was born on March 11.1954 in place Macea, Arad Country Romania Graduate of Economic University, Craiova Romania

1979-1989 Economist and Chief Economist and sales Department

In 1990-founding member of the first Parliament of Romania after the Revolution of 1989 in PCNU (Provisional Council of National Unity)

1992 - Independent candidate for deputy in the Romanian Parliament, Chamber of Deputies

1992-1996 Advisor to the Arad Country Council as an independent adviser

1992-1996 President of the Commission trade, tourism, services advise Arad Country Council

1990-2002 Director, manager of private companies wholesale

1980 - Philosopher and author books.

Ardelean Gheorghe Cornel(BIGAGC)

1980 He published 118 books, articles in publications, of which 50 English books and 68 books in Romanian

In 2009 - Member and Coordinator of Department programs, projects and activities of the non-profit. International Organisation Cornel Gheorghe Ardelean (OIAGC)

As a thought on long-term, positive, constructive, open, creative, humanistic, etc. It has a great ability to create so many positive ideas and solutions, constructive, humanist, creative, helpful people to achieve what they want. Thinking and ideas sustain and promote the rights of children, women, all people in the world, positive thinking and ideas, constructive, humanistic, tolerante, progressive, understanding and peace between peoples and nations.